The Astronomer's Garden

Beached

Two Plays by

Kevin Hood

For Pat

With thanks to Ted Craig,
Steve Gooch, Celia Bannerman
and Brian Matthews

Methuen Drama

A Methuen New Theatrescript

This collection first published in Great Britain in 1991 by
Methuen Drama, Michelin House, 81 Fulham Road, London
SW3 6RB and distributed in the United States of America
by HEB Inc, 361 Hanover Street, Portsmouth, New
Hampshire 03801.

ISBN 0-413-65080-4

A CIP catalogue record for this book is available from The
British Library.

The front cover is taken from the poster for the Croydon
Warehouse production of **The Astronomer's Garden**, copyright
© Paton Walker Associates Limited.

Printed and bound in Great Britain
by Cox & Wyman Ltd, Reading

Introduction

The words 'The Astronomer's Garden' first came into my mind on a walk through Greenwich Park when I found a little garden tucked away on the side of the hill under the Royal Observatory, an enclosed space with an atmosphere of secrecy and history. It felt like a theatre. I knew there was a play in it.

The title came first, the people afterwards, and first amongst these was Margaret Flamsteed, known to *his*-story solely as the wife of the first Astronomer Royal. She appears once or twice in the accounts, briefly illuminated on the edge of her husband's limelight. But these few appearances – her origin in a Surrey parsonage, a sharp letter or two, the plunder of the observatory on her husband's death – suggested a person.

I made the tourist's visit to Flamsteed's House and other characters began to appear alongside Mrs Flamsteed in the shadows. Characters left out of the official version because they were the wrong class, like the instrument maker; because they were the wrong sex, like Mrs Flamsteed; because they were the wrong class *and* the wrong sex; or because they were intellectually trivial, like the rake.

The garden I found on my walk was close to, but not exactly on the spot where 17th and 18th century astronomers took their breakfast. I am sure the Reverend John Flamsteed, first Astronomer Royal, would have abhorred the lack of precision I displayed in naming the place. I hope he would also have condemned the unverifiable mixture of imagination and history I twisted together to make the play. Especially the sex. Mr Flamsteed would not have wanted *that* in the story. That which most concerns us we force ourselves to ignore.

Place and sex are also important in the second play in this volume, *Beached*, and though the characters are very different – contemporary, South East London working class – they too find themselves dismissed as unimportant. Not by history this time, but by the power that runs society, the home and decides status within our culture.

The winners in this cultural game, that is the educated class, consider the language of such characters too feeble for the expression of high ideas and emotions, and those who speak it are often patronized or even derided. Tragedy in Catford being difficult to imagine without laughing.

But sparseness can charge language and stretch it to express subtle and complex emotions – this is the poetry of everyday speech. Whereas the highly developed, ornate language of the dominant culture is frequently employed for the exchange of pure nonsense. As to tragedy, we are all capable of that. Greek myths, for example, are part of everyone's psychological heritage – for better or worse.

Beached was my first play to receive a professional production. Out of pure ignorance I chose to write a two-hander because I thought it would be easier. I learned . . . slowly.

The Astronomer's Garden

The Astronomer's Garden was first performed at the Croydon Warehouse on 14 October 1988, with the following cast:

Dr Edmond Halley	John Arnatt
Sir Philip Anstey	Robin Sachs
Rev John Flamsteed	Frank Gatliff
Mrs Flamsteed	Emily Richard
Abrahams	Neal Swettenham
Lizzie	Charlotte Attenborough

Directed by Ted Craig
Designed by Michael Pavelka
Lighting by Richard Caswell

The play transferred to the Royal Court Theatre, London on 26 September 1989, with the following cast changes:

Dr Edmond Halley	Godfrey Kenton
Rev John Flamsteed	Trevor Baxter
Dr Halley's Servant	Marcus Powell

Setting

The year is 1717.

The play is set mainly in the garden and observatory-cum-house residence of the Astronomer Royal, in the royal park at Greenwich, which is on a hill overlooking the River Thames and City of London. There are occasional excursions to the back streets of London.

In the first production the play was performed in traverse. One side of the set, employed for the house and interiors, had two doors set into a wall with wooden flooring fading into grass. The other side of the set had a raised platform behind a line of wooden poles and this was used for the wilder parts of the park such as the Wilderness. The garden was the open green area between.

Prologue

The play opens with a dumb show.

A table set for work in the garden. In the middle of the table a heavy bound volume: Flamsteed's Historiae Coelestis Britannicae, *his famous catalogue of observations.*

English harpsichord music . . .

Halley *enters from the house side of the set, sees the book, steals across to the table.* **Flamsteed** *enters, sees him and walks quickly to reach the table just as* **Halley** *is about to grasp the book.* **Flamsteed** *clasps it to his breast and glares at* **Halley** *across the table.*

Anstey *enters and stands behind* **Halley**. **Abrahams** *enters and stands behind* **Flamsteed**.

Mrs Flamsteed *enters with* **Lizzie** *in the Wilderness side of the set and looks down on the tableau.*

Music ends. **Mrs Flamsteed** *speaks:*

These astronomers, their vision clear,
Look far beyond the human norm
Of hate and love, desire and fear,
Into pure reason, abstract form.

Minds like these are purged of error
By a myriad of scientific acts,
And Nature itself becomes their mirror,
Transformed by science, into facts –

Fragments of the universal plan,
Collected, catalogued and filed, by man.
Here the cosmic truths are served,
While the wounded child within goes unobserved.

Act One

Scene One

SFX: horses on cobbles.

A dark alley in London, 1717. Night. **Anstey** *strides on looking for a door.* **Halley** *follows.*

Halley God, where are we?

Anstey Somewhere east of Cripplegate.

Halley This place stinks.

Anstey All of London stinks, it's the shithole of the world.

Halley The roofs . . . hang so close you can't see the stars.

Anstey I've seen enough of them to last a lifetime. (*Turns slowly to face* **Halley**.) So . . . Africa.

Halley Yes, Africa. (*Beat.*) And very much more than you imagine.

Anstey (*turns away, laughing*) Oh, my imagination –

Halley This is more than sniffing alleys for whores. Or grubbing ditches for insects.

Anstey Spiders. (*Finds a door in the darkness.*) One of these I think.

Halley Wilderness is dangerous. It finds you out.

Anstey Very wise, Dr Halley, I'm sure, nevertheless, tell your friends I apply.

Halley (*pause*) Well.

Anstey Ah! This *is* it. (*Bangs on door.*)

Halley And my business?

Anstey Waiting only your letter of introduction.

Halley Waiting. I've waited years.

Anstey For a book?

Anstey *knocks even more loudly.*

Halley Eventually, Philip, as a man grows more mature these . . . these excursions lose their savour. Knowledge is a pleasure that lasts.

The door swings open. Lights pour into the dark street. A woman steps out. **Anstey** *holds her then offers her to* **Halley**.

Anstey What do you say to that?

Halley *shakes his head and turns sharply away.*

Halley Just get me the book. That's all I want.

Halley *off.*

Anstey But how? (*To woman.*) Flattery of course. The horticultural art. Sow the seed of respect, nurture it with esteem, and then – warm, liquid adulation in copious amounts. Something will come of it. Do you know that? Yes, you know that.

Slowly **Anstey** *pushes the woman backwards through the door as the lights come up.*

Scene Two

Rev *and* **Mrs Flamsteed** *are breakfasting in the garden of The Greenwich Observatory. She reads restlessly. He scratches at a paper with a quill, referring occasionally to a huge loose-leafed volume – his catalogue of the stars. He sips water and spits it out.*

Flamsteed Water? Miserable girl.

Mrs Flamsteed She's late.

Flamsteed Lazy slut. (*Tests air with pen. Sniffs.*) Pestilence.

Mrs Flamsteed What? Then go inside.

Flamsteed Rank inside. (*Writes.*) Cloud obscurity, 3 . . . 07 . . . till 4 . . . 11.

Mrs Flamsteed Then stay outside.

Flamsteed It creeps up the hill from the river.

Mrs Flamsteed A breeze. That's all.

Flamsteed The odour of pestilence is highly characteristic. It seeps in through the window night after night.

Mrs Flamsteed I never smelled it.

Flamsteed You've forgotten. Years since you observed. (*Beat.*) Never would have believed a woman had a mind for such matters. (*Beat.*) My bones ache.

Mrs Flamsteed Then why continue, night after night?

Flamsteed Because, madam, inconvenient though it may be, the stars only oblige at night.

Mrs Flamsteed Let Abrahams –

Flamsteed Abrahams observe without me? Never.

Mrs Flamsteed Well then. (*Reads.*)

Flamsteed *writes, a little arthritis makes it difficult.* **Abrahams** *enters with a letter on a silver tray.*

Abrahams This tray.

Flamsteed The milk's late, Abrahams.

Abrahams This tray.

Flamsteed The milk, Abrahams.

Abrahams This tray!

Mrs Flamsteed A letter? Letters are so rare here. Indeed, everything is rare here.

Abrahams Mr Flamsteed.

Mrs Flamsteed Always Mr Flamsteed.

Flamsteed *takes the letter.*

Abrahams (*being reasonable*) Sir. In the unexpected circumstance of William's abrupt departure.

Flamsteed (*opens letter. Reads.*) Halley again . . . Why should I see snotgobbler for you of all people Halley?

Abrahams May I remind you that I agreed to assist with the domestic duties . . . nothing undignified of course . . . for one day, just one day.

Flamsteed The servant gone? Is everything accounted for? My collected observations on variations in the moon's orbit in the tooled morocco binding? The catalogue?

Abrahams (*pointing*) There.

Flamsteed Oh . . . (*Finds the catalogue on the table before him.*) My study?

Abrahams Here's the key I locked it with at the end of a *very* long night of observation.

Flamsteed *is relieved.*

Abrahams This house needs a servant.

Mrs Flamsteed We have a servant.

Abrahams I am an astronomer.

Mrs Flamsteed Go and find the girl with the milk, Abrahams.

Abrahams *leaves defeated.* **Flamsteed** *reads.*

Flamsteed Can't afford to lose him. Too clever with his hands.

Mrs Flamsteed Too clever to work.

Flamsteed (*reading letter*) You don't give me instructions.

Mrs Flamsteed The domestic arrangements are my responsibility.

Flamsteed (*reads*) Halley. (*Explodes.*) I remember you. Strutting Cheapside like a cockerel.

Mrs Flamsteed Husband?

Flamsteed Mounting whores in the gutter.

Mrs Flamsteed *stunned*.

Flamsteed I'll publish when I have finished and not a minute before. God, let me finish, let me live to a hundred and spite them all.

Mrs Flamsteed (*pause*) Is that absolutely necessary?

Flamsteed Listen my instruments – they are to get nothing. No . . . wait . . . there's a box of broken pieces, let them have those with my compliments. It shall go in my will.

Flamsteed *scribbles*. **Lizzie**, *the maid, runs on with a jug of milk and pours into his mug immediately*. **Abrahams** *follows*.

Lizzie Milk girl was late. Run the whole way didn't spill a drop. Still warm. See? Later'n she's ever been. Can't help it. He'll have to do more. Do nothing all day long.

Abrahams I work nights.

Lizzie I work everythings.

Abrahams Ignorant skivvy.

Flamsteed *dips bread in milk, sucks it*.

Lizzie Say what he likes, it's only me. Mr Crow.

Abrahams Grubby little kitchen slut. Born in a ditch and dragged up in some stinking rat's nest of a cottage in the Godforsaken bogs of who knows where.

Mrs Flamsteed My home village actually.

Abrahams I am not a servant!

Lizzie What are you then?

Abrahams An instrument maker. A scientist.

Lizzie *and* **Mrs Flamsteed** *mock his dignity*.

Mrs Flamsteed We do not wish to hear the precise elevation of your position above that of the kitchen. Our science is not so exact.

Abrahams Sweet Jesus Christ, how much more of this must I bear?

Flamsteed Blasphemy!

Mrs Flamsteed Oh no.

Abrahams Mr Flamsteed –

Flamsteed In my garden. Blasphemer! (*Beat.*) Oh Lord God . . .

Flamsteed *waits until* **Lizzie** *and* **Abrahams** *sink, simultaneously, to their knees.*

Mrs Flamsteed The grass is wet. I've been ill.

Mrs Flamsteed *kneels reluctantly.*

Flamsteed We shall pray silently. With humility and love. For an indefinite period.

They groan. **Flamsteed** *kneels. They pray.*

Flamsteed Oh great Navigator of the Heavens who led the Israelites out of the Wilderness . . . send the longitude solution to me.

Mrs Flamsteed (*praying*) I can't bear this desolation. I'm dying day by day. Life! A child! Why do you deny me? (*Beat.*) Then the devil it is. Because I must have hope, I can't breathe without it.

Anstey *walks on and silently, mockingly takes in the scene. Walks over to* **Mrs Flamsteed** *and becomes serious for a moment, touched by her expression. Assuming a suitable expression himself, he kneels and prays in front of her.* **Mrs Flamsteed** *opens her eyes. They stare at each other for a long moment.* **Lizzie** *screams. They leap up astonished.*

Anstey Madam, forgive me – for, discovering you at your devotions I was inspired to my own.

They stare at him. He rises and approaches **Flamsteed**.

Anstey Sir. That fine intelligent cast of brow, the grey wisdom

in those eyes, surely none other than the Very Reverend Mr
John Flamsteed, Astronomer Royal. A great man is a beacon in
the world. I am honoured beyond expression.

Anstey *bows deeply*. **Flamsteed** *grunts*.

Anstey (*letter*) A letter of introduction from Doctor Halley –
your old friend in Science and Philosophy. (*To* **Mrs Flamsteed**.)
Madam, Sir Philip Anstey at your service.

Flamsteed *reads*. **Anstey** *turns to* **Abrahams**.

Anstey Mr Abrahams? The other Greenwich Astronomer.
Author of that notable communication: 'Preliminary
speculations on minor anomalies in orbits of some of the lesser
moons of Jupiter. A tentative suggestion'. How a man's mind
shines in his work.

Abrahams I . . .

Anstey Sir Isaac himself recommended it to my attention.

Abrahams Sir Isaac *Newton*?

Flamsteed They all came here once. Emperors, mathematicians,
that gaggle of pox-addled whores and pimps the old king –
Charles – wheeled up here every Sunday afternoon, breathing
their stink over the lenses. Sticky fingers on the brass.

Mrs Flamsteed Lizzie.

Anstey Lizzie?

Mrs Flamsteed Kitchen, Lizzie.

Lizzie *off*.

Mrs Flamsteed I must . . . Really, I must . . .

Mrs Flamsteed *off abruptly*.

Abrahams Sir Isaac Newton read my communication?

Anstey Indeed. He spoke the word: interesting.

Abrahams Let me die now.

Anstey Mr Flamsteed?

Flamsteed I will not be treated like a sight. Greenwich –
astronomer in the park – mustn't miss that. As to this. (*Letter.*)
You have been misinformed, Dr Halley and I are no longer
friends – in science, philosophy or anything else. This is my hour
for private study. (*Aside.*) Snotgobbler.

Flamsteed *off abruptly.*

Anstey What did he say?

Abrahams He said: interesting.

Abrahams *off, following* **Flamsteed**.

Anstey Well then . . . I can wait.

Anstey off.

Scene Three

Night in the garden, one day later. **Mrs Flamsteed** *on, she carries a
lantern and is dressed for bed.* **Lizzie** *asleep on the grass, a tray beside
her.*

Lizzie (*wakes at her touch, frightened. Shivers*) Ma'am? What you
doing out here this time of night? Not well yet.

Mrs Flamsteed (*sits*) Thinking.

Lizzie The observatory.

Mrs Flamsteed Sit with me.

Lizzie They'll be starving in there.

Mrs Flamsteed Appetite? My husband? He thinks of nothing
but his work. In the beginning I did too. I tried – sharpened
pens, copied endless observations. I was useful to him. Then.
Look at the city.

Lizzie (*trying to look*) So tired it's a mist.

Mrs Flamsteed Look at it glow. Mr Anstey will be there. (*Beat.*)

Don't you think his hands are beautiful? (*Beat.*) Have you been there?

Lizzie Don't need to go there to know what it's like, smell the stink from here.

Mrs Flamsteed They say the roofs hang so close in the old streets you can't see the stars.

Lizzie I'm a country girl, city enough here for me.

Mrs Flamsteed I never go anywhere, see anything, meet anyone. All I do is read books. What do they say – people, the people you meet, servants, tradesmen?

Lizzie Say pigs is more natural clean. Empty their pots on their own doorstep. Streets is ankle deep.

Disgusted together.

Lizzie All them people buzzin like shitflies round a midden – excuse me, ma'am. (*Conspiratorial.*) Whores in every shadow, worse.

Mrs Flamsteed Worse?

Lizzie Worse.

Mrs Flamsteed What?

Lizzie Just worse that's all.

Mrs Flamsteed Tell me.

Lizzie Don't want to hear it.

Mrs Flamsteed I do, I do.

Lizzie (*pause*) Men.

Mrs Flamsteed Men?

Lizzie *Men.* Wherever you look, wherever you go – eyes, words, hands. A woman who walks them alleys 'lone better watch herself close, I tell you, or it's pulled off into the dark and then what, eh?

Mrs Flamsteed What, Lizzie?

Lizzie And God, so brazen. Lookin' up and shoutin' out and askin' on with them *questions*, or smarmin' round with them smiles all over their stupid faces. Know what they want, though. Tongues hangin' out for it.

Mrs Flamsteed What . . . exactly?

Lizzie Sniffin' after it like dog after bitch. And more'n half with red, runnin' sores which is somethin' very bad.

Mrs Flamsteed But how do you know if you haven't been?

Lizzie That's what they say, people I meet. Besides, same in Greenwich.

Mrs Flamsteed But that's only the lower classes. Surely a man like Mr Anstey –

Lizzie Eyes. Hoss trader's look.

Mrs Flamsteed Lizzie!

Lizzie Food to take in.

Mrs Flamsteed No, not yet. Don't leave me. (*Beat.*) I can't sleep any more. Look how thin I've become. I nearly died.

Lizzie Didn't though.

Mrs Flamsteed You helped me. (*Takes her hands.*) Rough hands.

Lizzie And yours so soft.

Mrs Flamsteed My little friend from the village. We might almost be sisters.

Lizzie Imagine that, soft hands. (*Dozing.*)

Mrs Flamsteed (*looks towards observatory*) You know, sometimes I imagine . . . my husband . . . the body under his clothes, grey meat crawling with maggots. This place is breaking my heart. (*Pause.*) Go on Lizzie. Go on.

Lizzie *is asleep.*

Scene Four

Anstey *waits in the garden, passing time with restless swordplay.*

Anstey One day – indifference, insult. (*Stops.*) But I will not be provoked. Siege . . . (*Lunges.*) . . . wins more wars than battles. So wait. Just wait. And . . . wait.

Lizzie *struggles on with a basket of washing.* **Anstey** *plunges his sword into the basket. The washing spills in the mud.*

Anstey *Touché.* Is the proper response.

Lizzie Look at that.

Anstey More work, and so much to do already.

Lizzie Dirty. Look at it.

Anstey Poor . . . Lizzie?

Lizzie Drag it here, drag it there. Now look at it. Drag it back again.

Anstey Poor little fingers. (*Takes her hands.*) Sore little fingers. Poor, rough –

Lizzie What?

Anstey – raw, unthinking little Lizzie. Apple cheeks and soft brown eyes.

Lizzie Eh?

Anstey Is there somewhere near? Not the usual place. You are clean by the way?

Lizzie Do the best I –

Anstey (*pulls her*) Come on then.

Lizzie Where? (*Realisation dawning.*) No . . .

Anstey Lizzie!

Lizzie (*pulling away*) No!!

Anstey No? Ah. Forgive me. (*Beat.*) You see, I'm shy. I am not one of those to whom words come easily. Please, forgive me, because – (*Throws himself to his knees.*) I am conflagrated.

Lizzie Confla . . . ?

Anstey To a crisp.

Lizzie Mad.

Anstey With love. And all for you.

Lizzie This time in the mornin'?

Anstey Yes. For some subtle reason the soft magic of the night is lingering.

She backs away.

My mind is a mist of enchantment. Strange perfumes run wild amongst my senses.

Lizzie I heard about this. (*And backs . . .*) But I didn't believe it.

Anstey Sweet nymph . . .

Lizzie Till now.

Anstey I kiss your knees in worship –

Lizzie No!

Anstey No?

Lizzie No!

Anstey No magic? Sure?

Lizzie Sure.

Anstey Then . . . (*Spins a coin.*) Silver. Real enough for you? However science has proved it dissolves in mud. (*Spins money to the ground.*) Did you know that?

Lizzie Go on.

Anstey Ever see silver lie in mud?

Lizzie Never see it reach the ground before.

•

Anstey (*more*) Five shillings. Six. Seven. Melts clean away. Like churchbread on your tongue.

Lizzie *is fascinated by the money.* **Anstey** *gets behind her and pulls up her skirt. She struggles to escape.*

Lizzie No! Off! I'll scream.

Anstey And they'd blame you. You'll starve.

Lizzie Still do it. (*Gets free.*)

Anstey Virtue?

Lizzie *picks up the washing and goes.*

Anstey In a kitchen slut? Where's the sense in that?

Anstey *extracts his sword from the basket. Waits.* **Lizzie** *back on. Tries to put washing back into basket.* **Anstey** *won't let go.*

Lizzie I'm a servant not a whore.

Anstey You're a slut.

Lizzie (*pulls*) Basket.

Anstey And in my experience sluts are often dribbling idiots but never your kind of fool.

Lizzie Basket.

Anstey Virtue is always for sale. Seven shillings in the mud or an earldom.

Lizzie Only trade then?

Anstey There's nothing 'only' about trade, it's pure biological reality: kill, eat, fuck.

Lizzie Well silver's not my price.

Anstey Then what is?

Lizzie Nothin' you'd spend. And it's my right to say.

Anstey A slut's rights are what a master can't get away with.

He advances on her, but she fends him off with the basket and escapes.
Anstey *sprawls.* **Flamsteed** *on.* **Anstey** *discovers himself watched.*

Anstey Specimen hunting. Spiders.

Flamsteed Insects?

Anstey Spiders aren't insects. Arachnids. Devised the name myself.

Flamsteed Not insects?

Anstey (*recovers*) A common enough misunderstanding.

Flamsteed I assure you that when I misunderstand I do so in a most uncommon manner. Spiders, insects – equally trivial.

Anstey Shouldn't a scientific interest be diverse?

Flamsteed Scrabble from one half-digested morsel of knowledge to another like . . . an arachnid? No. Painstaking experiment, endless calculation, decades and decades . . . until slowly, even very slowly, something of lasting significance emerges.

Anstey Exciting.

Flamsteed (*produces a blindfold*) In the day I rest my eyes for observation. You have had the best of me.

Anstey (*pause*) I understand Dr Halley –

Flamsteed Newton's creature, and Newton is a thief.

Anstey The greatest man of the age?

Flamsteed Bad breath and extravagant condescension.

Anstey Gravity alone –

Flamsteed Anyone can have an *idea*, but you need measurements to prove it. In this case, precise observations of the moon's orbit provided by me. In short, gravity is mine though he has stolen the glory. And what does he want this time? Hmm? Do you know what the positions of three thousand stars is? A map of the universe. A mathematical net to catch the farthest reaches of reality. And guide the king's ships into profit.

Anstey Longitude?

Flamsteed Yes. Mine. King Charles gave the commission to me. (*Beat.*) Solve it for me, he says. But that will require a map of the entire universe. Do it, he says. Clocks and books and instruments. Get them, he says. And somewhere to live. Build it, he says, you . . . you shall be my Astronomer Royal. Titles, Sir Philip, are cheap. The tricky sod paid me once in fifty years.

Mrs Flamsteed *bustles in.* **Lizzie** *follows with a tray.*

Mrs Flamsteed No horse. So it had to be a walk. Also long, therefore you will need refreshment. Logic is very popular here. Lizzie!

Flamsteed Logic?

Mrs Flamsteed Amongst the Moors, the lady of the house serves an honoured guest.

Mrs Flamsteed *gestures and* **Lizzie** *puts down the tray.* **Mrs Flamsteed** *pours wine.*

With her own hands. (*Stares at his hands.*) I read it. In a book.

Flamsteed (*drags the blindfold off.*) Moors?

Mrs Flamsteed You will eat with us at midday? I insist.

Flamsteed Eat?

Mrs Flamsteed Pardon my husband, Mr Anstey, a lifetime of logic but a minute of politeness? – never. You may find he improves a little as the day progresses.

Anstey I'm sure –

Mrs Flamsteed Are you? I wish I was. About anything. Mr Anstey, I read book after book but only the poetry makes sense.

Flamsteed (*to his wife*) Sir Philip. *Sir* Philip.

Mrs Flamsteed Oh . . . Oh . . .

Mrs Flamsteed *off abruptly. Then back on.*

Inexcusable.

Mrs Flamsteed *off*. **Lizzie** *follows*.

Flamsteed Are you afflicted with a wife? Cheaper than a housekeeper but infinitely less convenient.

Anstey The Royal Society –

Flamsteed Halley has bastards everywhere you know.

Anstey Really? And Doctor Whiston?

Flamsteed Brains like stewed porridge.

Anstey Doctor Whiston has devised a method for discovering the longitude.

Flamsteed (*laughs*) Discovering the longitude.

Anstey The Admiralty is examining the proposal in the Bay of Biscay at the moment. A full-scale trial.

Flamsteed (*laugh trails off*) But the opinion of the Astronomer Royal? My book?

Anstey No stars in it.

Flamsteed No stars?

Anstey Irrelevant.

Flamsteed But I've spent fifty years on stars, I have the most comprehensive collection of stars in the history of science.

Anstey It's all rockets now. Whiston's method is ingenius. Let me explain. Ships, specially designed for the purpose, are anchored at known positions of arbitrary longitude along all the sea routes. And fire rockets at regular hours throughout the day and night.

Flamsteed Rockets?

Anstey Not just rockets, *new* rockets . . . which always and without exception explode at a known, fixed height – very important that – and are intended to be observed on the navigating ships. The method is, as you will have gathered, triangulation. Distance to the rocket burst is calculated from the time between flash and report, the angle subtended is measured with a sextant, a brief calculation and then . . . no more sugar cargoes on the reefs, no more pirates waiting on familiar latitudes to net the gold and spice of the India Fleets. In other words – the freedom of the seas.

Flamsteed (appalled) Longitude. (*Forces himself to speak.*) I must have rockets. The distance from here to Shooter's Hill where I measured the speed of sound. Abrahams! We must measure the exact height, variability that's the weakness. Abrahams! Can you get me . . . a new rocket? The Whiston method for longitude! – I'll pay anything.

Anstey I do have friends in the Admiralty. But it will take time.

Flamsteed Sir, I am in your debt. Abrahams! (*Rushing off.*) Abandon everything. The world has gone mad.

Flamsteed *off*. **Anstey** *pleased with himself*. **Mrs Flamsteed** *on*.

Mrs Flamsteed Sir Philip.

Anstey Madam.

Mrs Flamsteed Your title. I should have known. Nobility is . . . intrinsic.

Anstey Gentry – I am a baronet.

Mrs Flamsteed It should have been obvious to me.

Anstey Madam, please –

Mrs Flamsteed Do you know *The Song of Solomon*?

Anstey Sheep and goats and so forth?

Mrs Flamsteed Eyes like the Pools of Hebron.

Anstey And what are they?

Mrs Flamsteed Deep. (*Beat.*) I would like to show you the park. It's very famous. King Henry rode here with Anne Boleyn.

Anstey Oh dear.

Mrs Flamsteed (*missing the joke*) Sir John Vanbrugh is building a house, over there, so they say. Would you like to see?

Anstey Building work?

Long pause. **Mrs Flamsteed** *can't proceed.*

Madam, few things give me more pleasure . . .

Anstey *offers his arm. Continues speaking as they walk off.*

. . . than contemplating the spectacle of a new and impressive erection.

Scene Five

Anstey, *drunk, walks into the candlelit backroom in a brothel where* **Halley**, *sober, is waiting. Harpsichord music and the laughter of women in the background.* **Anstey** *takes a whore in his arms and is momentarily philosophical.*

Halley How much longer must we wait?

Anstey You know, when I was a child, the girl who put me to bed. Her skin was miraculous. (*Beat.*) Twelve years old. Of course, my mother . . . Ever talk, I mean really talk to a whore?

Halley Yes, your mother.

Anstey They understand everything. The eyes . . .

Halley The cheap scent, the stale sweat.

Anstey Every trade stinks, and what a trade. Cunt for collateral. Her survival, my pleasure.

Halley The waste, spending yourself in sluts like these?

Anstey I will have you know, father, I intend to address my entire being to the exclusive pursuit of noble ideas and great thoughts.

Anstey *fondles the whore.*

When I'm too old to do anything else.

Halley These parasites. Amoral monkeys living on the carnal weakness of men. Skin smooth, soft . . . warms under your fingertips. The mane of hair, the greedy little mouth opening up for more, always more. It is an abyss! Nothing becomes a man like the study of natural philosophy.

Anstey Cheap scent for me, the cheaper the better.

Halley And then?

Anstey And then perhaps I'll be less inclined to sermonising my bastards than you, father. Especially when they whore in your service! You astronomers talk nature – all celestial machinery and ethereal mathematics, but it's much more real than that. Nature is kill, eat, fuck. Power. Who kills, who eats, who fucks!

Halley You are your mother's son. So much at least can be proved.

Anstey Doctor Halley's comet may twinkle in the heavens, but in the drawing rooms of London, a more socially significant place after all, my mother is nothing less than incandescent.

Halley An object of extraordinary luminosity. Was there nowhere else we could meet this man!

Anstey So disapproving. And why? I'm not in debt, not much. Dead drunk no more'n five nights a week. Not poxy, which is pretty good since I fuck everything I see and quite a few things I don't. Exemplary. Your obligation, sir, your obligation . . . is discharged.

Halley I refuse to meet you like this again.

Anstey And I refuse to look through your telescopes again.

Halley *moves angrily to go. Stops.*

Halley What do you really want?

Anstey Not Astronomy. (*Beat.*) Africa.

Halley We've decided. Two years.

Anstey Two years! The voyage –

Halley Misery, slugs in your water, maggots in your breakfast . . .

Anstey Some discomfort –

Halley Unspeakable! And when you get there? A fringe of pestilential coastline and a great white wilderness on the map. Africa, send in explorers and madmen come back.

Anstey But think of the specimens.

Halley There is that.

Anstey Two years. I'll go mad without women.

Halley Sailors?

They laugh.

Stay here and work with me.

Abrahams *led in by the whore.*

Anstey Ah, Mr Abrahams.

Abrahams Sir Philip. There are so many rooms in this house. And so many strange things going on in them.

Anstey May I present my uncle Doctor Edmond Halley, Secretary to the Royal Society. We have been discussing your excellent work.

Abrahams *and* **Halley** *meet.*

Abrahams Doctor Halley, I can't describe how I feel. The honour.

Halley Your instruments are famous.

Abrahams My paper.

Halley Your paper?

Anstey 'Speculations on anomalous perturbations in some orbits of certain of the Moons of Jupiter, a hesitant outline'.

Anstey *and* **Halley** *work together at conning* **Abrahams**.

Halley (*to* **Anstey**) Have I read your paper?

Anstey Hasn't everyone?

Halley (*beat*) Indeed.

Anstey Sir Isaac.

Halley Enthralled. Captivated. The best . . .

Anstey Short communication.

Halley Since . . .

Anstey Hooke's pump.

Halley Hooke's pump?

Abrahams Hooke's pump! Sir Isaac, *himself*?

Anstey Word is sent from Cambridge. He wishes to be considered your friend. Think of it – evening sunlight in your crystal glass, conversation with the greatest man of the age, and finally, cool crisp linen emblazoned with the monogram of your own college.

Abrahams *sinks into a chair. The naked woman steps out of the darkness to fill a glass. He doesn't notice her for a moment, and is then startled.*

Anstey An excellent rendezvous, don't you think? Who would expect men of our character to meet here. And secrecy is vital.

Halley (*impatient*) Sir Philip assures me you are a man on whom one can rely for . . . subtlety of understanding. (*Beat.*) Flamsteed.

Abrahams Flamsteed!

Halley He is Astronomer Royal, I am Secretary of The Royal Society, the star catalogue is therefore our property.

Abrahams *begins to be worried.*

Anstey (*to* **Halley**) Slowly, Uncle.

Halley (*ploughing on*) But he is determined to publish everything himself, become the most famous astronomer in the history of mankind. Grotesque! The catalogue won't get him longitude, that'll be solved by a good clock. Its true value is scientific.

Abrahams, *increasingly worried by the turn of events, drinks absent-mindedly. The woman leans across him to fill his empty glass.*

Abrahams You want me to . . .

Halley Stars, planets, moons, comets, thousands of observations, that is the real treasure.

Anstey Why settle for Flamsteed's lackey when you can be Newton's friend? In Cambridge.

Halley (*realising*) Cambridge?

Anstey (*pause*). Yes. Still unconvinced?

Abrahams It is his life's work. His reason for living.

Anstey *fills* **Abrahams**'s *glass*.

Anstey More wine?

Lights crossfade to next scene.

Scene Six

The garden. Afternoon.

Lizzie *carries a joint of meat to the table.* **Anstey** *traps her.*

Lizzie You.

Anstey Sir Philip, slut.

Lizzie Sir Philip, sir.

Anstey Better.

Anstey *prevents her when she tries to move.*

Lizzie You have the advantage of me, sir.

Anstey Irony?

They dodge round the table.

Lizzie God, I'm sick of this.

Anstey It won't be long then. And not before time. In this house my erection is permanent.

Lizzie If she could hear you.

Anstey But she never will.

Lunges across the table, misses her.

Silver words for her. But for you the metal. Your arse in the mud and me revolving between heaven and earth.

Lunges again. She pushes him back.

Lizzie Look at me!

Anstey I do. I do.

Lizzie Look like my mother. Life drained out. More like her every day. I'm bone tired.

Anstey I know. I know.

Lizzie Look at my face.

Anstey Beautiful.

Lizzie For how long? Livin' twice as fast as you. Be old before you're finished being young. (*Beat.*) Everything you are depends on me. Wear out my life energy buildin' yours up so's you can chase me round this table. Jesus. Enough gals like me in the world, same face, same arse and ten times more in the way of it.

Anstey We have come to a measurement.

Lizzie Why do you torment me like this?

Anstey (*laughs*) What do you gain by this virtue?

Lizzie I'm tied.

Anstey The road. You're free.

Lizzie Eat grass on the way, live like a pig when I get wherever it is?

Anstey Take a little money with you.

Lizzie I want more than that. (*Beat.*) Can't go, not on me own, cause there's . . . men like you wherever I turn.

He lunges and she fends him off with the meat. He is left holding the joint as **Mrs Flamsteed** *comes on. He assumes a philosophical pose.*

Anstey (*pause*) Consider madam, the flesh this once was. How it moved like we move, felt like we feel. Is this the end we too shall meet?

Mrs Flamsteed Excuse me?

Anstey Philosophy.

Mrs Flamsteed Philosophy? (*Beat.*) I have been thinking. (*Beat.*) I was alone a great deal as a child, no one . . . brought up a heathen, in a rectory, isn't that strange?

Anstey Knowing rectors . . .

Mrs Flamsteed And it's so quiet here. Real life impinges so little. As to real life . . . Lizzie and I live very quietly. Don't we, Lizzie?

Lizzie Yes ma'am. Very quietly.

Mrs Flamsteed Lizzie is my friend. Almost. (*Beat.*) And I read a great deal. Books. But there are many things I don't understand, lacking, as I do, so much experience. Of the world and . . . so forth. Matters such as . . .

Lizzie *and* **Anstey** *hang on her words.*

Honour. An important idea. Ruling a person's life. Men *talk* about it all the time, at least they do in books, but what does it mean? And for a woman? I sometimes think I don't believe the things I should. I mean, how far should – Of course I *know* the answer to that but . . . (*Beat.*) It makes me think of the statues in the gardens of the Queen's House. Down there. Striking attitudes in the bird muck. (*Giggle.*) Should I have said that?

Anstey These statues, their attitudes are amusing?

Mrs Flamsteed Yes, very. (*Beat.*) Lizzie?

Lizzie The meat, ma'am.

Anstey *puts the meat down.*

Anstey Show me? But you must promise not to tell anyone what I say. I warn you, it may not be conventional.

Mrs Flamsteed *and* **Anstey** *off.* **Lizzie** *works.*

Lizzie Attitudes, how they wear me down. God, let me be free of this place.

Abrahams *on.* **Lizzie** *furiously busy then rounds on him.*

Lizzie Skivvy one minute, astronomer next. Where do you belong, Mr Crow?

Abrahams Cambridge University.

Lizzie What?

Abrahams And then my own parsonage. Just for the living of course and so much as cannot be avoided in the way of obligatory duties. The country is infested with irregular parsons, one more won't even be noticed . . . Somewhere near somewhere. I shall need the company of others of my own kind. Members of The Royal Society.

Lizzie He says?

Abrahams He says.

Lizzie Believe him?

Abrahams I . . . don't know.

Lizzie Parson? Well you're miserable enough. What else though? Parson needs some sort of sense. You got no more'n a scarecrow. What's under here? (*Coat.*) Straw?

He pulls away, trembling at her touch.

Lizzie (*pause*) What you looking at? Dirt on my face? Wash off, bit of a lick. See, white, just like them. (*Beat.*) Statues.

She poses. He looks.

Course this dress is fair worn through now. Look at it. See. So thin. Don't get money 'nuf for proper dresses. Can't expect to look more'n I do. Except for Sundays. Sundays I always look . . . you seen me Sundays, Jonathan now haven't you just?

Abrahams Lizzie . . .

Lizzie Can't talk to you when your eyes go everywhere. (*Beat.*) We're the same, you and me.

Abrahams You're a servant.

Lizzie I know exactly what I am, and exactly what you are. A whore.

Abrahams Whore?

Lizzie And cheap. Pride, that's all they pay you. Just feeling a little better than you are. Oh, too clever not to know it. Listen. You're a whore, so be a whore, but be a good 'un.

Abrahams (*trying to move away*) I'm going to Cambridge.

Lizzie *comes close.*

Lizzie We're the same you and me. Look, you don't know me yet. Quiet. Wait. Still. Mouse in the shadow. Till the time's right. And the time is right.

Long pause. She is close, he doesn't move away.

Need a wife in Oxford.

Abrahams Cambridge.

Lizzie Still need a wife. Work hard, you seen that. And I can learn to speak different. Learn fast. Won't open my mouth till the words are polished like glass. (*Beat.*) You look at the stars and I'll make pies. I make good pies. (*Beat.*) And I am beautiful. When you look at me. And you do look at me. Out the corner of your eyes. Seen you. Looking. When you think I'm not. Beautiful. People say so. And I'm young and strong and Oh God I'll die, I swear I'll die, I will *die* if I don't get safe soon and away from this place.

Abrahams It's unbearable.

Lizzie No more.

Abrahams No.

Lizzie Start fresh over. You and me.

Touches him. He trembles, but does not pull away. She continues.

All that waiting. Has been for this. And there's never been nobody else, Jonathan. Nobody, ever. Soft under that starch, yes?

Abrahams Oh.

Lizzie Ain't this what you want though?

Abrahams I . . .

Lizzie Me? You want me? I can feel it in your arms. Hold me.

He can't move.

Tinder dry. All piled up for a spark. So when does your fire start?

Abrahams *bursts into flame.*

Abrahams Lizzie.

Lizzie Hey . . . hey . . . hey! What you saying?

Abrahams Saying? Saying? What am I –

Lizzie What do you want?

Abrahams Y . . . y . . .

Lizzie Come on, say it.

Abrahams You.

Lizzie That's right. Me, me.

She kisses him.

And freedom. Do you hear it in the woods at night, smell it in the mornin' 'fore the day turns sour? Parson needs a wife, yes? (*Beat.*) We're the same, you and me, yes?

Abrahams Yes.

Lizzie *Yes.* And I'll change, seem right, I will. (*Curtsies.*)

Abrahams Yes.

Lizzie That's right. That's what I am. Wife, right?

Abrahams *stands trembling, overwhelmed by emotion.* **Lizzie** *disengages slowly. She returns to the table, works. He approaches.*

No. Not yet.

She moves to go off, turning to look at him before she goes.

(*Aside*) That's it then. Mrs Crow.

Lizzie *goes off.* **Mrs Flamsteed** *and* **Anstey** *come on.* **Abrahams** *is left standing as Flamsteed comes on.*

Flamsteed Where are my tables?

Flamsteed *and* **Abrahams** *sit and work.* **Abrahams** *is uncharacteristically tardy in responding to* **Flamsteed***'s needs. The conversation shifts between them and* **Mrs Flamsteed** *and* **Anstey** *at the other end of the garden.*

(*To* **Abrahams**.) Calculate to the second decimal place . . . five miles . . . take into account the curvature . . . (*Across the garden to* **Anstey**.) Aristotle saw motion as a horse pulling a cart, we see it from the muzzle of a gun.

Mrs Flamsteed Do you have an avenue of chestnuts on your estate, Sir Philip?

Anstey Limes.

Flamsteed And a regular increase in the propulsive force.

Mrs Flamsteed (*indicating the observatory.*) At first, King Charles wanted a ruin here, with an ape-house but he settled for an observatory instead . . .

The others are calculating.

. . . with an astronomer. (*Beat.*) Why *build* a ruin?

Anstey Fashion. Grotto myself, and a hermit – fifteen pound a year.

They smile. **Anstey** *walks to the other end.*

Flamsteed Sir Philip. My theory is already well advanced. But I am badly in need of the rocket. It's been a week.

Anstey Very soon. Tired, Mr Abrahams? Then rest.

Abrahams No rest for the wicked.

Anstey *picks up* **Abrahams**'s *tables and walks away.* **Abrahams** *must therefore follow.* **Mrs Flamsteed** *is restless.* **Anstey** *watches her as she stretches herself.*

Anstey (*to* **Abrahams**) Women have deceit like cats have claws. But rather a cat than a dog any day, always licking your hand or biting it. Lick or bite, Mr Abrahams?

Abrahams He gave me my opportunity.

Anstey And you gave him your talent.

Abrahams How can I repay him by stealing his work?

Anstey Nothing is stolen unless Flamsteed steals it from the world. What he does is for us all or it is valueless.

Anstey *returns to Mrs Flamsteed.*

Mrs Flamsteed Do you love nature?

Anstey Love? No, not love, I'm interested in it.

Mrs Flamsteed Oh my husband is *interested*.

Anstey But only in the precise position of stars, comets sailing through infinity, all that.

Flamsteed (*snaps his fingers*) Tables.

Anstey And this obsession with numbers. Mathematics is a sophisticated form of anxiety. Abstraction – preferably at an enormous distance. But the reality? The bloody mess of being alive right here in this garden terrifies them. The truth is we are animals, all of us, and we live by the same rules, though we dress it up a little with God and morals for show.

Mrs Flamsteed So cynical, so blasphemous?

Anstey Everything worth saying is cynical or blasphemous. Look at how people are. Why do they really map the stars? Longitude – trade – money – *power*. Exactly how spiders would behave, given a bigger brainpan.

Mrs Flamsteed The cynic and the scientist, a cold world for you both. You can't love it because you're disappointed in it.

Anstey What? (*Beat.*) No. Interested, as I said. (*Walks away.*)

Flamsteed (*really getting into it*) Ballistics is the study of the modern age. Path through the atmosphere. Shape of the missile. Air resistance. Take a feather, take a guinea. Look how they fall.

Does just that. Then returns to calculation.

Anstey (*to* **Mrs Flamsteed**) Truth is this garden and its infinite, microscopic variety.

Mrs Flamsteed And people?

Anstey People? Yes, they interest me. Though not quite as much as spiders.

Mrs Flamsteed Well, I quite see that interest is preferable to love in the case of a spider.

Anstey In his web – just as alive as you and I, just as aware in his own way. The silk in his grasp, the soft ripples of tension he catches the world with. Very much alive, and all around us now. Killing, eating . . . continuing his species.

Even more restless, **Mrs Flamsteed** *walks to the far end of the garden.*

Mrs Flamsteed (*points*) Look.

Anstey A butterfly?

Mrs Flamsteed A blue.

Anstey Seven English blues, I have them all.

Mrs Flamsteed Isn't it beautiful?

Anstey Seventeen reds, I have sixteen.

Mrs Flamsteed Will you show me?

Anstey If you wish.

Mrs Flamsteed Yes. I wish.

Flamsteed Ink! More ink!

Abrahams *moves to get the ink,* **Anstey** *moves to intercept him.*

Anstey You move slowly. A very cautious man.

Abrahams The fruit of a practical education. I was a watchmakers' apprentice when I was eleven.

Lizzie *enters with her basket, watches them, then goes.*

For something to work, everything must fit together in my mind first, cogs mesh and turn without a click or a hitch. Always got to see it in my head first, and working, or I can't start. For someone like me miracles are almost as hard to swallow as humble pie.

Anstey You need a little faith.

Abrahams When Doctor Halley is accused of Atheism?

Anstey Don't be small-minded, the Anglican Church is broad enough for that. Tell me, how did *she* get to be with *him*?

Abrahams His country living by all accounts, left behind in the attic with the other lumber when the previous rector died. He just picked her up where she was left off.

Flamsteed Ink!

Abrahams *off.* **Anstey** *turns to find* **Mrs Flamsteed** *gone. He is left with* **Flamsteed**, *who has succeeded with his calculations.*

Won't work. Sir Philip! (*Sits back and thinks.*) You know, never been satisfied with the notion of Gravity myself. Touch of magic about it. Invisible forces pulling across space. Weak idea.

Stops calculating.

(*To* **Abrahams** *off.*) How long must I wait? . . .

Lights crossfade. Runs into next scene.

Scene Seven

Observatory. Night. **Anstey**, **Flamsteed** *waiting. Behind, a telescope mounted on a quadrant.* **Abrahams** *is with the instrument.*

Abrahams I'm doing it as fast as I can.

Flamsteed (*to* **Abrahams**) Get going, get going! You've got work.

Abrahams The gallows?

Flamsteed On Shooter's Hill. There's a corpse. The stink will help you find the place in the dark.

Abrahams *off.*

Anstey How will the rocket be lit?

Flamsteed A long pole with a lighted match.

Anstey Well, he certainly does work, does Abrahams.

Flamsteed But so slowly.

Anstey He'll get there.

Flamsteed I know the distance to an inch – learn the value of an inch, Sir Philip.

Anstey I hope he's careful with my horse. Doesn't hurt her mouth.

Flamsteed He's not good with horses.

Anstey Won't be long in getting there then.

Flamsteed *adjusts the quadrant.*

Flamsteed Hurry Abrahams, hurry! Reliability is essential for maritime navigation. One failure will give me all the ammunition I need. The new quadrant . . . Old fingers, should have got him to set it. Delicate business.

Anstey He's clever then.

Flamsteed With his hands. Telescopes, clocks, navigational devices – oh, beautiful instruments. Could make a guinea a week in business for himself. But as to understanding, slow. Wants to be an astronomer! Ha! There, Whiston's 6440 feet exactly. Measurement is the bedrock of practical mathematics, and mathematics is truth. Remember that.

Anstey (*looks through telescope*) May I?

Flamsteed (*loudly, as if* **Anstey** *is an idiot*) In the sights. We see it explode there. At that precise angle or the method's a failure. What does Whiston know about navigation? Breeds carrots in his backgarden.

Anstey (*mainly to himself*) Poor Abrahams. What a difficult night: wild horse to get him there, corpse stinking on the gallows where he must work, and the rocket – (*Laughs.*) could go anywhere at all.

Flamsteed The calculations rely on the same thing happening every time. It's impossible – the charge must be correct to one grain of powder, the powder absolutely reliable, and the fuse precisely the right length to explode at exactly, *exactly* 6440 feet.

Anstey Cold enough to freeze up a French tart.

Flamsteed (*looking out*). Clear skies. Hope the cloud holds off. I measured the speed of sound up here with your friend Halley. He sat on the gallows and fired the pistol. I measured the time between flash and report. Calculated the speed before he walked back. Furious to be left out. That was the night he revealed his true character.

A whistle blows in the distance.

Listen.

Once . . . twice . . . Prepare yourself!

Far off, a rocket whooshes. There is a flash and a second or two later the sound of an explosion.

Anstey Well?

For a long time, **Flamsteed** *stares through the sights of the quadrant.*

Mr Flamsteed?

Flamsteed The quadrant, the quadrant, the angles must be wrong. They must be.

Frantically he examines the quadrant before slumping backwards.

6440 feet. Oh . . .

Anstey (*genuinely surprised*) Really?

Flamsteed To the inch.

Anstey Remarkable.

Flamsteed To the inch!

Anstey The value of an inch, eh.

Flamsteed Whiston!

Anstey Yes. The Whiston Method for longitude.

Flamsteed I'll be damned as a Cheapside pimp before I'll have it. (*Struggling.*) This could be . . . a lucky chance?

Anstey Perhaps.

Flamsteed (*struggling for control*) What we have seen tonight is clearly . . . impossible. Both theoretically and technically . . . quite impossible.

Anstey It happened.

Flamsteed But in a larger sense . . . in the proper context . . . (*He thrashes round.*) An accident of mathematics.

Anstey An accident? Is truth subject to accidents?

Flamsteed Oh, it must be . . . (*Thinks furiously.*) Statistics! Yes. (*He's found it.*) One . . . *one* explodes at 6440 feet perhaps but others . . . burst on the ground, shoot sideways, backwards, and those few that do struggle into the skies . . . explode at every height *except* 6440 feet. (*Pause.*) We must be objective. You won't mention this?

Anstey Premature.

Flamsteed (*anxiously nodding agreement*) Premature.

Anstey Yes.

Flamsteed Not to Halley, please not to Halley.

Anstey Oh no, not to him.

Flamsteed (*collects himself*) A series of experiments has become necessary. I must have more rockets.

Anstey I will try, but it will be difficult.

Flamsteed I'm in your hands.

Anstey Yes. It'll take a week.

Anstey *and* **Flamsteed** *off.*

Scene Eight

Mrs Flamsteed *runs up to the wall of the garden and prowls, looking anxiously out.* **Lizzie** *follows with broom.*

Mrs Flamsteed Sometimes he comes by the river.

Lizzie Showing yourself.

Mrs Flamsteed Can you see him?

Lizzie Look . . . men like him . . . you don't understand how they go on.

Mrs Flamsteed (*hands over her ears*) I can't hear this.

Lizzie We mean nothing.

Mrs Flamsteed Stop! Or, I'll send you back.

Lizzie No. I looked after you. You need me.

Mrs Flamsteed You are not capable of understanding Sir Philip and myself. (*Beat.*) We talk, we discuss, we . . . share certain sensibilities. It is a matter of education and sensitivity. Affinity. (*Grabs* **Lizzie**'s *hand.*) Please.

Lizzie (*pause*) Whatever you say, Ma'am. Bread's in the oven.

Mrs Flamsteed Don't go. I . . . (*Moves in various directions.*) He may need to stay. After the observation. Lizzie. The other room.

Lizzie Full of things.

Mrs Flamsteed Clean it out. I wish I'd thought of this before. Keep the books. Dust them. A goosewing for books, it says so in 'The Wife's Companion'. He will know the books are mine. Mr Selkirk, Mr Defoe, Mr –

Lizzie Books is full of dangerous things.

Mrs Flamsteed You can't read?

Lizzie Spiders. Big as your hand.

Mrs Flamsteed Country girls aren't afraid of spiders.

Lizzie (*aside*) Learn to read though. My own books. Own plates. Own linen. Own rooms. Too much work here. But nobody listens.

Mrs Flamsteed I'll get women from the town. This house is to be *transformed*. I think it will be the river with all those rockets. Oh. He's here.

Mrs Flamsteed *sees* **Anstey** *walking up the hill. She struggles to compose herself.*

Mrs Flamsteed He's here. (*Fluttering wildly.*) At least the table linen is good. Fine brown Holland. Don't serve.

Lizzie Always serve.

Mrs Flamsteed But not tonight. We'll get people up from the inn. That will be all I need. Stay in the kitchen, Lizzie. (*Beat.*) Your eyes shine in the candlelight.

Lizzie I know.

Anstey (*voice off*) Look out! The pony has more sense than you.

Abrahams *bustles past with a copy of the catalogue.*

Lizzie (*aside*) Well?

Abrahams Almost done.

Lizzie Jonathan, we're going tonight.

Abrahams But –

Lizzie Has to be. Everything's happening so fast.

Abrahams I need more time.

Lizzie Tonight! Finish it.

Abrahams *off*. **Anstey** *on, with his specimen box.*

Anstey These people. (*Shouting off.*) Careful! Drop one of those and we'll all ride it back to London. Rockets are the most unpredictable things on earth. Or I used to think so.

Mrs Flamsteed You came by the river?

Anstey Yes. (*Beat.*) My compliments, Madam.

Mrs Flamsteed You brought your specimen box.

Anstey The butterflies.

Mrs Flamsteed May I see? – Lizzie, the kitchen. – Show me.

Lizzie *off*. **Anstey** *unpacks his box*. **Mrs Flamsteed** *looks*.

Anstey Of course butterflies are not my major interest.

Mrs Flamsteed *examines the collection, slowing down as it gets larger and larger.*

(*Pause.*) You don't like them after all.

Mrs Flamsteed (*pause*) They're . . . dead. They're all dead.

Anstey Well, yes. What did you expect?

Mrs Flamsteed I just thought I might see things your way.

Anstey The collection is . . . pretty complete, as far as the British Isles are concerned. Though very limited in range compared to Africa.

Mrs Flamsteed Africa?

Anstey Yes. (*Beat.*) There is an expedition . . .

Mrs Flamsteed Africa! (*Pause.*) When are you leaving? Soon?

Anstey Yes.

Anstey *packs away. Silence.*

Mrs Flamsteed I didn't mean to offend you.

Anstey Rest assured, madam.

Mrs Flamsteed (*pause*) How long?

Anstey Two years.

Mrs Flamsteed Two years! (*Gasp.*) My husband, I'll . . .

Anstey There's enough time for him. Don't go . . . Tell me . . . How did *you* come to be *here*?

Mrs Flamsteed My husband . . .

Anstey Let him wait.

Mrs Flamsteed My husband and I were married. (*Pause.*) My grandfather, was a clergyman, had a living in Surrey and when he died there was nowhere else to go. One day Mr Flamsteed walked into the garden, stood on the lawn, looked around – I can remember the moment exactly – I was watching from the trees. Black shoes in the grass. He saw me. It seemed he was my guardian and then somehow he just sort of . . . took me over with the rectory.

Anstey Lock, stock and granddaughter.

Mrs Flamsteed Everything seemed to belong to him. There were debts as well, I suppose.

Anstey And you paid them. God. I am going tonight. It must be tonight. After the test I really must go.

Mrs Flamsteed (*pause*) I know. (*Beat.*) But the deer. I haven't shown you the deer. You said you wanted to see them.

Anstey One does.

Silence.

Mrs Flamsteed What shall I do now?

Anstey Show me the deer, of course. We have time.

Mrs Flamsteed Two years?

Anstey Yes. Let me say something, let me . . . (*Beat.*) Mrs Flamsteed, I don't care how I appear to the world, only to myself. I can't go on being this dilettante for ever. Beyond a certain age . . . Africa will set up a little order in this unruly mess. Change me. Make me a scientist. My career as a cynic is about to end.

Mrs Flamsteed Yes. (*Beat.*) The deer. Give me . . . a little time.

Mrs Flamsteed *off.* **Anstey** *almost stopping her.*

Anstey Well, what would you do with her? You know what you are.

Lizzie *on.*

Spying, kitchen slut? You know what I am too.

They stand and stare for a moment and then jump: he for her, she away.

Bitch. Don't play with me.

Lizzie No games. Just there's a time and a place.

Anstey Ah!

Lizzie And a price. Everything to be fixed like I said.

Anstey I never haggle, it's beneath my dignity. How much?

Lizzie Stay where you are.

Anstey Very wise. I don't trust me either.

Draws his sword, guides the point into his stomach and the hilt into her hand.

One lunge and I'm disembowelled.

Lizzie And I'm hanged.

Anstey They'll say he died for love.

Lizzie We've had all that.

Anstey (*money*) And this?

Lizzie Gold. All that?

Anstey And another.

Lizzie The devil tempts.

Anstey Well, I am in flames.

Lizzie Why'd you pay that for me?

Anstey Because you smell like her. And you are beautiful.

Shuffles forward with the sword still in place.

Because beauty is power. You'd own me given the chance, any woman would. But what I buy is mine to dispose of. Run me through if you have to but – Jesus Christ.

Anstey *nicks himself on the sword, jumps back.* **Lizzie** *falls down.*

Just a nick. Oh.

Goes down on his knees at the same time as throwing coins into her skirt, chinks the coins. She fends him off.

Listen, listen. All you have to do is open your legs and help. (*Sings.*) Tom, Tom the piper's son / He learned to play when he was young / But the only tune that he could play – / was over the hills and far away. Oh, sorry, but you are going to have to kill me.

She shuffles backwards on her bottom, he follows on his knees.

Here and now.

Lizzie Not here.

Anstey *laughs and stops.*

Lizzie And twice, twice this.

Anstey I've never paid half before.

Lizzie For the help. And because I smell like her. Tonight.

Anstey I'll be with Flamsteed.

Lizzie Best time. Creep away. Trees, bottom of the garden.

Anstey You sure you're a virgin?

Lizzie I'd know.

Anstey And so would I. Don't try to cheat me.

Lizzie (*manoeuvring to stand up*) You're an handsome man and words like a mouthful of birds when you've a mind. But you're a bastard all the same.

Anstey Bastard? And yes, that is exactly what I am, but are you a virgin?

Abruptly he brushes the sword aside and examines her with his hand, brutal, a sort of rape. Then silence. It is uncertain if he will go further. But the garden is too exposed after all, he sheathes his sword and goes off. **Lizzie** *leans on the specimen box and stands up again.* **Mrs Flamsteed** *on.*

Mrs Flamsteed Has he gone?

Lizzie Yes, he's gone.

Mrs Flamsteed He's leaving for ever. Tonight.

Lizzie Good riddance. Bastard.

Mrs Flamsteed *slaps* **Lizzie**. *Silence then –*

But he loves you. He told me so. Loves you.

Mrs Flamsteed Told you?

Lizzie So sweetly. And I've seen it in his eyes, the way he looks at you when you're not looking. Affinity.

Mrs Flamsteed But he is leaving!

Lizzie Oh, this isn't just low class riffraff, this is a man of honour. He'll be thinking of your reputation, ma'am. (*Beat.*) Course, the thing is, are you going to let him go?

Act Two

Scene One

The park near the wilderness.

Lizzie *and* **Abrahams** *on.*

Lizzie Will you finish it?

Abrahams Three more pages.

Lizzie When?

Abrahams Later, after the rockets. Plenty of time. We have the rest of the afternoon. What happens now?

Lizzie Not sure.

Abrahams *grabs her.*

Lizzie No! Don't paw me, right! Don't handle me like that.

Abrahams You touched me. God and how.

Lizzie We wait. And maybe, just maybe it'll be worth the waitin' for. You managed so far.

Abrahams Oh . . . I was an ascetic then. Discipline, cold water, long cool calculations. But now, *now* – you can't imagine what's going on in my head, it's the fall of the Roman Empire in here. Desire – years and years of it building up and suddenly it's bursting all over the place. I am staggering with lust. My senses have gone wild. I can't keep still. I dance. Abrahams *dances.*

Lizzie Turned out human after all then.

Abrahams Please.

Lizzie Don't beg. Too much of your trainin' in it. Step up like a man and ask nice if that's what you want.

Abrahams (*does*) Well, Lizzie?

Lizzie Elizabeth, that's my given name.

Abrahams Elizabeth . . . (*Grabs her again.*) Make love on the grass – warm air on your skin and blue sky brimming in your eyes? Will you?

Lizzie No.

Abrahams God!

Lizzie That gets said to everybody. Find me a word. You know lots of words, find one for me.

Abrahams Love?

Lizzie No, somethin' real. Like respect, like . . .

Abrahams Dignity?

Lizzie Oh yes, like that – dignity.

She takes his hands and wipes them on his own coat.

Dry hands. And what do I go to Cambridge as?

Abrahams As?

Lizzie The words, want to hear them said properly. My given name. Dignity.

Abrahams We *are* the same you and me. Elizabeth, will you consent to be my wife?

Lizzie (*pause*) Why should I do something like that?

Abrahams Because . . . unless we work together you'll be skivvy and I'll be scribbler in Flamsteed's cold, dark house for the rest of our lives. Right then! So! I am Anstey's whore. The book is almost ready. I'll whore for Anstey, and that old bastard? Let him rot. I'll be an astronomical parson and you'll be an astronomical parson's wife.

Lizzie Ask me, ask me properly.

Abrahams *on his knees.*

Abrahams Elizabeth Jennings, I ask you to share my life, success and failure, triumph and tragedy, profit and loss.

Lizzie Well, there's a start.

Abrahams Only a start?

Lizzie Long way to go before I make you and me real in my head.

She goes off. He follows. **Anstey** *and* **Mrs Flamsteed** *on.*

Anstey Wilderness?

Mrs Flamsteed The wildest place in the park. Do you believe some places are special? I know every shadow here. A leaf quivers and I feel it. Flowers open and close, feel the sun and rain and I feel it with them.

Anstey Very nice.

Mrs Flamsteed No one ever understands.

Anstey Is it safe?

Mrs Flamsteed Sometimes at night men bring dogs and lights. They understand fear. They take everything, even the fawns.

Anstey You have actually *seen* it?

Mrs Flamsteed When they're in the nets, all tangled up, and the dogs – I feel so powerless. You'd feel the same. I know you would. I'll show you the deer and then you'll know. But you'll have to be quiet. They don't trust men.

Anstey I can be quiet.

Silence. They sit, listen. **Anstey** *fidgets.*

Anstey Woods are never silent.

Mrs Flamsteed Not with you in them.

They settle.

Anstey I know how to behave.

He fidgets again.

Mrs Flamsteed Find me a spider.

Anstey *searches.*

Now I understand the knees of your breeches.

Anstey *has no success.* **Mrs Flamsteed** *lies back.*

I could float off on this breeze.

Anstey You play, you play like a child. Forgive me, but for you this is some sort of show put on for your entertainment. All this benevolence! (*Beat.*) In America, or somewhere equally exotic, there is a spider that has its mate build a web, allows herself to be invited in, submits to his supplications and at the very climax, the very pinnacle of ecstacy . . . buries her poisoned little sting in his heart, bites off his head and sucks the twitching body dry.

His search has brought him very close to her.

That is nature too. (*Beat.*) Any other stretch of woodland in England – I could lift a spider in ten seconds.

Mrs Flamsteed Except here.

Anstey Except here.

She opens her hand and shows him a spider. She drops it into his hand and they touch with a shock of contact.

Mrs Flamsteed Some places are special.

Anstey I am going to Africa.

Mrs Flamsteed I know.

Anstey I must.

Mrs Flamsteed Yes.

Anstey There's no difficulty with specimens there. In fact I have never experienced any difficulty with specimens anywhere before. Why is it suddenly so awkward?

Mrs Flamsteed I don't understand.

Anstey Sometimes you do, sometimes you don't. Your confusion confuses me much more than – what am I saying?

Mrs Flamsteed I don't –

Anstey Oh. All this innocent sensibility. Do you paint watercolours of natural scenes by any chance? Do you embroider flowers or anything like that?

Mrs Flamsteed No.

Anstey No. You're not obvious, more's the pity. Strange to find oneself suddenly moral – I was thinking of the deer.

Mrs Flamsteed Shush.

They look at the deer.

Hasn't seen us. Don't breathe.

They start together as it flits away.

Oh . . . So light on their feet.

Anstey No one has told them about gravity.

Mrs Flamsteed Lucky things. I hear about it all the time.

Anstey Your husband would not approve of deer.

Mrs Flamsteed I've never asked him to. (*Beat.*) Let's go deeper.

Anstey I am leaving. Tonight.

Mrs Flamsteed (*unable to move*) Let's go on.

Anstey When I was a child there was a girl. Saw far more of her than dear mama. She looked after me. Sometimes when we were away from the house and no one could see, or at night in my room when she put me to bed, she let down her hair. Long black hair glistening in the candlelight. Let me see.

Anstey *is letting down her hair. She trembles violently but can't move.*

Mrs Flamsteed A child.

Anstey It is beautiful.

Mrs Flamsteed You're leaving. Oh.

Anstey Yes. I must.

Mrs Flamsteed I . . .

Anstey Margaret.

Mrs Flamsteed I . . .

With a great effort of will, **Mrs Flamsteed** *gets herself to her feet and forces herself to leave. But only just.*

Anstey Mrs Flamsteed. (*Pause.*) Africa. I feel I'm already there. (*Beat.*) What was it? It finds you out. Well, out, out, *out*. Tonight.

Scene Two

The observatory. A candle in the darkness. A clock ticks. **Abrahams** *copies furiously from* **Flamsteed**'s *copy of the catalogue. Finishes.*

Abrahams Done it!

And hurriedly stuffs it into a ready sack which he hides. He pretends to be asleep. **Flamsteed** *enters.*

Flamsteed Everything hangs by a thread and you sleep. Nothing is prepared.

Wakes **Abrahams** *up. Checks instruments. Arrested by a thought.*

How long have I been doing this? (*Beat.*) My first observatory –

Abrahams Tower of London. Ravens. Shitting on telescopes. I know, I know.

Flamsteed In the beginning . . .

Abrahams *mouths it with him.*

I was forced to take in pupils. Aristocracy! Lavish more care on their dogs than on their sons. Run 'em wild and then expect mathematics to teach 'em proportion. Well, I taught geometry with a pen in one hand and a whip in the other. How long have we observed together?

Abrahams Ten long years.

Flamsteed Settings?

Abrahams As instructed.

Flamsteed Good. (*Shivers.*) So cold. The body, always demanding.

Abrahams Yes. Demanding and demanding.

Abrahams *belches.*

Flamsteed The air in here is foul enough already without you.

Abrahams That pie . . .

Flamsteed Pie?

Abrahams Tender, yielding meat. Oh – sensation! Where have I been all my life?

Flamsteed You are full of yourself tonight. (*Beat.*) Do Anstey's men know what to do? Everything must be exact.

Abrahams They are trained seamen.

Flamsteed Ignorant louts pressed at gunpoint.

Abrahams Well, yes. Who serves without necessity?

Flamsteed You do. (*Notices his hands.*) Abrahams . . . why are your fingers so particularly stained with ink?

Abrahams Ten years of copying. It's ingrained.

Flamsteed Is Anstey reliable? Can we trust Halley's friend?

Abrahams Absolutely, we can trust him absolutely.

Flamsteed*'s moment of suspicion passes.*

Flamsteed Good mind but it lacks direction. Grubbing about in the woods! (*Beat.*) Fifty years, my catalogue still incomplete, and I'm waiting for a firework party.

Flamsteed *moves to telescope.*

Flamsteed I will show him. After the rockets Sir Philip and I will observe together. Then he will be able to compare. Newton! 'I was sitting in the garden one day and lo . . .' That apple has stuck in my gullet for years. But I have it from a friend whose gardener once spoke with a boy who worked in the grounds of Newton's house they had blight that year. History will see me right. My book will eclipse all the lesser lights. Yeah, even Newton.

Anstey *on with specimen box. He joins* **Abrahams** *and* **Flamsteed** *around the telescope. Cramped.*

Flamsteed Sir Philip.

Anstey Mr Flamsteed. (*Aside, mouthed.*) Well?

Abrahams (*mouthed*) Done.

Flamsteed Are the men reliable?

Anstey Totally. (*Aside, mouthed, behind* **Flamsteed**'s *back.*) Give it to me. (*To* **Flamsteed**.) The view from up here is remarkable, even at night.

Anstey *and* **Abrahams** *contrive to manoeuvre the bag, the book and its contents into the specimen box over the next several lines of dialogue, bumping into* **Flamsteed**, *stopping when he notices and resuming when he turns away.*

Flamsteed This afternoon, you were in the park with my wife.

Anstey (*stopping – a new difficulty*) Yes.

Flamsteed Tell me . . . can *you* understand what she says?

Anstey (*manoeuvring*) We talked about the deer.

Flamsteed Only interesting thing about deer is their taste. How can this be happening? Fifty years and my entire reputation resting on this grotesque experiment. It will not happen!

Anstey *and* **Abrahams** *successfully complete the transfer of the copy to the specimen box.* **Anstey** *puts the box on the floor.*

What's in that box?

Anstey Box? Specimens.

Flamsteed Specimens?

Anstey Spiders, butterflies.

Flamsteed Still on with that? I'll show you something better than –

The first rocket goes up. They measure the burst.

Oh . . . Oh . . . Oh . . . OH!!! Straight. High. Abrahams?

Abrahams *calculates.*

What is it? Hurry!

Abrahams About . . . 6000.

Flamsteed But not 6440?

Abrahams 6400 feet.

Flamsteed What?

Anstey Amazing.

Abrahams Close.

Anstey Very close. And I was told the first could be the weakest.

Flamsteed This is a nightmare. Reset the quadrant. (*Irascible.*) Come on. Slow-witted . . . Incompetent . . . workman.

Abrahams *slowly stops what he is doing, looks at his hands.*

Abrahams Workman.

Flamsteed Do what you're told. Now!

Abrahams Workman. Well, yes. Ten years. Telescopes, lenses, clocks. My skill for your knowledge. Years I've worked for you and you have, I must admit, shown me a great many things. But courtesy has never been one of them. I'm leaving.

Flamsteed Leaving?

Abrahams This very instant.

Flamsteed You can't leave me now. The measurements.

Abrahams Measurements? I have my own to make. The workman will work for himself.

Abrahams *sweeps out.* **Anstey** *has enjoyed the scene.*

Flamsteed Piss on you then! (*To* **Anstey**.) You and I. We'll observe the next together. Please be so good as to assist –

Anstey The next? (*Backing out.*) If you don't mind, Mr Flamsteed, I will observe that from the garden. A breath of fresh air. Specimens.

Anstey *gone before* **Flamsteed** *can stop him. His specimen box is left behind.*

Flamsteed Sir Philip? . . . Spiders. Butterflies. (*Looks at specimen box.*) Mechanical bugs, meaningless toys. Where is truth in that?

Flamsteed *walks over to the box and lifts it up. Pause. Blackout.*

Scene Three

Garden. Darkness. **Lizzie** *in her dayclothes is packing a bundle.* **Abrahams** *enters.*

Lizzie Well, has he got his book?

Abrahams Copied. Finished. He won't stay long now. Oh, my eyes haven't closed for a week.

Lizzie What happens next?

Abrahams They'll write to me.

Lizzie Anything could happen and what could we do about it?

Abrahams We can trust him.

Lizzie Ho!

Abrahams He's a gentleman. He'll keep his word.

Lizzie We'll have to trust him, we got no choice. But I'm still not stayin' here beyond the night, whatever happens.

Abrahams We aren't ready to go yet.

Lizzie Changing your mind?

Abrahams No. But what about my books? I sweated blood for them.

Lizzie Pack them now. Hide them somewhere and come back later. Anything!

Abrahams It doesn't have to be tonight. We can wait.

Lizzie Made up my mind to it, that's all. Can't bear another minute.

Abrahams *goes to embrace her.*

Be top of the park waitin' for me at dawn or I'll go on my own. I'll stay with the milkgirl till then.

Abrahams Where will we go?

Lizzie Don't matter where. (*Beat.*) Yes it does. (*Beat.*) Cambridge. They can't turn us away now, not after what you done. Get on their doorstep and make them pay.

Abrahams I have no money. I never cared about it before.

Lizzie Because you wanted to be an astronomer in a fine black coat.

Abrahams I will be an astronomer.

Lizzie How much did Flamsteed pay you?

Abrahams A pittance.

Lizzie How much could you earn making clocks?

Abrahams My clocks? Guinea a week, more.

Lizzie As much as that! And he gets it free. People like us. They take our life, energy, spirit, flesh off our bones like it belonged to them. This house is famous, it'll be remembered. But who'll remember us? (*Beat.*) I got the money we need. Saved up. And we start tomorrow. Make our way village to village on the trader's carts.

She is suddenly terrified.

Abrahams What's wrong?

Lizzie Touch me now. Hold me. Gently. My face is burnin'. Oh God. I hope all this is worth it.

Abrahams You're trembling. Why?

Lizzie My mother. Her face.

Abrahams What?

Lizzie Only saw her cry the once – day I left home come here. We was halfway down the lane – me in the cart, her walkin' alongside in the mud – and all of a sudden she just stops. Stock still. And then she's goin' back from me, right. And then her face . . . hard, grey, and tears. (*Beat.*) Like rain washin' stone. (*Beat.*) Watchin' me die if only I knew it. Oh God I knew it. It's not happenin' to *me*. Hold me tight. Ain't never had a man. That way. You believe me? Kitchen slut that's never been touched, imagine that.

Abrahams Yes. I can imagine that. I'll wait. It'll be worth it.

Abrahams *embraces her.*

Lizzie Good. Better get back. Things to do. Pack what you can carry.

Abrahams And the rest?

Lizzie Bury it.

Abrahams Anstey.

Lizzie *off.* **Anstey** *on.*

Anstey You have done well, Mr Abrahams. The good Doctor Halley will be pleased. Ambition is whispering in his ear. From Secretary to President of The Society and after that, Astronomer Royal. You could be very useful then.

Abrahams Here?

Anstey It would be different.

Abrahams Never.

Anstey And in the meantime you could keep us informed as to developments – in his health especially . . .

Abrahams No, no question, I must go. When will I hear?

Anstey (*beat*) When Dr Halley writes.

Abrahams Now you've got what you want?

Anstey You are doubting my word?

Abrahams I'm going to Cambridge. Write to me there. At Sir Isaac's college.

Anstey (*pause*) As you wish.

Anstey *draws his sword and pins* **Abrahams** *at the throat.*

Though I really should kill you for the insult, you know.

After a pause, **Anstey** *sheathes his sword.*

I do hope the book is worthy of my restraint.

Abrahams (*relieved*) Three thousand stars.

Anstey A skyful.

Abrahams Your rockets will be going soon.

Anstey If the sailors aren't too drunk to light them. (*Beat.*) Christ, I am so tired of telescopes and clocks and instruments.

Abrahams Mr Flamsteed will be waiting. He wants you to observe with him. Like a real astronomer.

Anstey All night?

Abrahams Usually.

Anstey Not tonight. Have you seen the maid?

Abrahams Lizzie?

Anstey Where is everyone?

Abrahams I've got things to do. I'm leaving.

Anstey So he's all on his own. Oh dear.

Anstey *off. Lights change to . . .*

Scene Four

Halley *lectures to the Royal Society at the beginning of an evening. He has bottled specimens of human brains before him.*

Halley Gentlemen . . . (*Introductory remarks.*) The human brain. A mystery. On the one hand, part of the body corporeal. On the other, seat – we are told – of the human soul.

Bottled specimens are held up by a **Servant**.

Man and woman. It is said – men think, women feel. (*Displays a female brain bottled in preserving fluid.*) Note the smaller cranial capacity of the female, the limited development in the higher regions here, reminiscent of the rudimentary brain of the ape – might we not speculate a failure of development? Has it not been established that girl-children are produced by debilitated sperm? So, what is the force that pollutes this concentrated power of man's perfect being? (*Demonstrates a male brain, then puts it aside.*) We must look to the point where form intersects with flesh. Remember – these same few pounds of tissue that discovered mathematics are home of the foulest, most depraved imaginings of which a human creature is capable.

A **Servant** *puts a spotless apron on him.*

Some men live to feed their minds and conserve the energy of their vital fluids for husbanding thoughts rather than wives. Others live in a whirlpool of lasciviousness, dissipating their energy as carelessly as they make their secretions, and the end of that is a stagnant pond of seminal weakness. When the male element of pure form mingles with the female element of base matter, the one must slowly be degraded by the other.

Examines his dissecting kit. Puts on his spotless white gloves.

But we are scientists and aspire. Nature and her mysteries. The centuries-old veil of ignorance and superstition. It is this and this alone we strive to lay bare, and desire . . . to penetrate.

Scene Five

Night. The garden illuminated by a great number of stars. **Lizzie** *pulls* **Mrs Flamsteed** *on. They are both wearing nightclothes.*

Mrs Flamsteed No . . . I'll lose everything.

Lizzie Lose what?

Mrs Flamsteed I mustn't. I mustn't.

Lizzie When he's gone. Be like before.

Mrs Flamsteed But how can I?

Lizzie Easy.

Mrs Flamsteed For you.

Lizzie And you.

Mrs Flamsteed Look at me.

Lizzie Remember the wood.

Mrs Flamsteed But that wasn't here.

Lizzie Happened though. Like it was intended. The spider. His hand to yours. You told me.

Mrs Flamsteed That was the wood, that wasn't here.

Lizzie This is the way he'll go. Out of the door, across the lawn, through the gate and you'll never see him again. Who'll know? (*Beat.*) Wait for him in the shadows.

Mrs Flamsteed *makes a dash.* **Lizzie** *catches her.*

Never see him again, the rest of your life. Make him stay.

Mrs Flamsteed It is wrong.

Lizzie Living wrong? Breathin' wrong? Wait here.

Lizzie *lets go of her. She stays.*

Mrs Flamsteed What do I say?

Lizzie Think of something. From books. That should hold him.

Mrs Flamsteed Books?

Lizzie Say what you feel then.

Mrs Flamsteed Can't think.

Both terrified.

Lizzie Steady. A little fright and a little time to get over it and then *he'll* know the rest.

They wait.

Come on. Christ! Come on.

Mrs Flamsteed It's too exposed. The light.

Lizzie Stars that's all.

Mrs Flamsteed What if someone sees.

Lizzie In the shadow. As thin as the air you breath.

Mrs Flamsteed I'm going to be sick.

Lizzie Oh no.

Nearly sick. But isn't.

Thank God.

Mrs Flamsteed How do I look . . .

Lizzie Beautiful.

Lizzie *lets down* **Mrs Flamsteed**'s *hair. Then her own.*

In the starlight.

Mrs Flamsteed What will I say?

Lizzie Tell him how you feel.

Mrs Flamsteed And what happens then? (*Beat.*) Is it true? What they said in the village. How can that be true?

Lizzie Don't you ache to know? Be here soon.

Mrs Flamsteed It's wrong. I lose everything. Please . . .

Lizzie Wait till he sees you in the starlight. He loves you.

Mrs Flamsteed I know.

Lizzie Listen. Whose voice do you hear? Whose voice?

Mrs Flamsteed You.

Lizzie Listen then, I know what you want.

Lizzie *touches* **Mrs Flamsteed***'s hands, she is trembling.*

You're burnin' . . . Hands, arms – burnin' . . . Feel the blush all down your neck.

Mrs Flamsteed Please.

Lizzie You been kissed?

Mrs Flamsteed No.

Lizzie Ever?

Mrs Flamsteed No.

Lizzie Not even that? Not even once?

Mrs Flamsteed Never, never, never, *never.*

Lizzie *kisses her.*

Lizzie Like that?

Silence.

Touched?

Mrs Flamsteed No.

Lizzie *takes* **Mrs Flamsteed***'s hands and puts them on her own body.*

Touch then.

Lizzie *touches* **Mrs Flamsteed***'s body as she speaks.*

Here. And here. And his hands are so much softer than mine. And what they know, eh? All silk and cream and fire.

Mrs Flamsteed God forgive me. I –

Lizzie Too late for that now. Feel your blush clear head to toe.

Mrs Flamsteed Please . . .

Lizzie Here. Now. Wait in the dark. Wait. *Wait.*

Mrs Flamsteed *just off in the darkness.* **Lizzie** *gets up quickly as* **Anstey** *comes on. He is on the other side of the stage, and carrying a candle.*

Anstey Lizzie? Is that you?

Lizzie Waitin'. Like I said.

Anstey Well then.

Lizzie *keeps her distance moving around outside the candlelight.*

Lizzie Well then. Put out your light.

Anstey Come closer.

Lizzie Stars. That's all we simple country girls need.

Anstey Your eyes shine in the candlelight.

Lizzie I know. Put your candle out.

Anstey That's a job for you.

Lizzie You first, then me.

He snuffs the candle. Stars bright.

Anstey Look at them. I've a book with thousands in. Just numbers. Page after page of numbers. What he calls the essence of reality. But it is nothing like this.

Lizzie Money?

Anstey My practical little amateur.

Lizzie Want to see the gold.

Anstey Good. Everything out in the open.

Anstey *tosses the money onto the lawn.* **Lizzie** *circles. He tries to find her and catch her. The money stays in the centre.*

Lizzie Not here.

Anstey Come and get your money, Lizzie. This is the time. So close I can smell you.

Lizzie Dog and bitch on the lawn?

Anstey Dog and bitch. On the lawn. A little animal reality to restore the balance. Too much philosophy gives me an erection. Everything gives me an erection. Stop dancing.

She makes a dash for the money. He grabs her.

Here we are then. You and me. Skin and sweat.

He sets about her from behind. Desperately, **Lizzie** *scrambles away from him in* **Mrs Flamsteed***'s direction.*

Lizzie Too . . . Too light. In the . . . dark.

Anstey Where you are.

As he attempts to do this, **Lizzie** *escapes to the darkness, meets* **Mrs Flamsteed** *and spins her off balance. From behind,* **Anstey** *captures* **Mrs Flamsteed** *and pushes her face down to the ground. Immediately* **Anstey** *engages* **Mrs Flamsteed***, who is at first silent, then moans with pain.* **Lizzie** *watches.*

There you are – At last!

Lizzie *off.*

Anstey Oh! Oh! (*He comes. Long pause.*) Well then. Very sudden. Never mind. Lots of time. In a little while, we can –

He turns her over. A rocket bursts overhead. Long silence. Another rocket bursts.

Anstey Something of the character of a mistake has been made.

Mrs Flamsteed I . . . You were very abrupt.

Anstey Yes . . .

Mrs Flamsteed (*in pain*) I didn't know . . . what to expect.

Anstey No.

Mrs Flamsteed I mean, I've never . . .

Anstey Never?

Mrs Flamsteed I didn't know, Philip . . . Will there be a child? I'd like a child with eyes like yours. When I first saw you I thought of the Song of Solomon – remember, eyes like the pools of Hebron. (*Beat.*) I can't believe it. I want to touch your hands. I've always wanted to touch your hands. I can do that now, can't I?

Anstey A child is by no means certain.

Mrs Flamsteed (*disappointed*) Oh.

Anstey In fact there are measures . . . I did not mean this to happen.

Mrs Flamsteed I know. But it happened. (*Touches herself, pain.*)

Anstey This was a mistake.

Mrs Flamsteed Don't call it that. How can it be – I came here. For you. It was brave of me.

Anstey Yes.

Mrs Flamsteed You and – the woods, the deer, the spider – we saw those things the same, yes, yes?

Anstey Yes, but –

Mrs Flamsteed But? You feel the same. I know. (*Beat.*) The same?

Anstey The same.

Mrs Flamsteed Then where is the mistake?

Anstey The mistake is that you were in the garden. (*Beat.*) No! I will not allow myself . . . The same? No! Everything in control, clear, fixed, in control.

Silence.

Mrs Flamsteed I don't understand. How can you deny what you did?

Silence. A rocket bursts.

Anstey I didn't know.

Mrs Flamsteed (*beat*) Don't go, Philip. Don't go! Oh my – not yet, please. A moment longer. Oh God, please not – a moment longer . . .

Mrs Flamsteed *is struggling hard to hang on.*

What is happening to me? Philip? It could not be that I am this much mistaken in you. Touch me.

Anstey (*pause*) I can't.

Mrs Flamsteed Why not?

Anstey I can't.

Mrs Flamsteed *Why not?* You love me. Deny it.

Silence.

Philip?

Abrahams *comes on carrying the specimen box.* **Lizzie** *behind, very much at a distance.* **Mrs Flamsteed** *tries to reclaim a little of her dignity but is appallingly exposed.*

Abrahams The catalogue. It's . . . He found it, smashed everything. I'll have another opportunity to copy it. He depends on me too much to send me away. I'll do it again.

Anstey *opens the box. He takes out torn pages of the book. Underneath, his specimens – destroyed.*

Anstey What?

Mrs Flamsteed *picks up a leaf of paper. And then another.*

Abrahams I can restore everything. A little time that's all I need.

Flamsteed *on. A rocket bursts. Silence as he takes it in.*

Flamsteed Bastard! Snotgobbling bastard!

Mrs Flamsteed You love me. I *know* you do.

Anstey Margaret . . . (*Pause.*) Margaret . . . Ha. What does it matter.

Anstey *sees* **Lizzie**.

You've done well, Lizzie.

Lizzie Elizabeth.

Anstey My congratulations.

Anstey *almost off, but can't stop himself from striking* **Lizzie**.
Abrahams *knocks* **Anstey** *to the ground, dragging out his sword and making a great wild sweep that just misses killing him.*

Missed me! Missed your opportunity. Forget Cambridge, forget Newton, forget your own little parsonage. Forget everything.

Abrahams *holds the sword about to strike.* **Anstey** *thinks he is about to die.* **Abrahams** *throws the sword aside.*

Flamsteed You betrayed me. All of you.

Abrahams So . . . it's over is it? My ridiculous hopes. Well, take your astronomy then, take it! Science, parsonage, gentleman – take it all! That's gentry for you. (*Meaning* **Mrs Flamsteed**.) Lizzie, we're going all the same. It's a guinea a week for me. And then more. I can do things. Make things. Lizzie!

Lizzie (*to* **Mrs Flamsteed**) Got to go. I got to go with him. Way it is. Learn. And then forgive.

Abrahams Look out for me.

Abrahams *off with* **Lizzie**.

Mrs Flamsteed The way it is? I was not meant to be like this. We were meant to be together.

Anstey You'd own me.

Anstey *picks up his sword, packs the remains of his specimens into their box.*

Mrs Flamsteed I know what you feel. Trust yourself.

Anstey You'd have me in the palm of your hand.

Mrs Flamsteed Don't go! Don't go! When you go, the world will end.

Anstey *goes.* **Flamsteed** *and* **Mrs Flamsteed** *are left.* **Mrs Flamsteed** *rushes past him, out of reach of his hand. His eyes follow her, burning with hate.*

Scene Six

Halley *lectures, having just finished dissecting. His apron and hands are bloody. The* **Servant** *helps him change into his fine clothes.*

Halley Well, we are what we are. Animals perhaps, but something sets us above nature. There are those, even here, who would say – feeling. No, no, no. Just think of the weaker sex, prey to every whim and casual depravity. Not feeling. Civilisation exists through government *of* emotion not *by* it – in women, in savages, in the lower classes and, most especially, in ourselves. We must look elsewhere. (*Beat. Gloves and apron off.*) Man alone possesses the unique capacity for rational thought. We can know the world . . . in order to master it. Wilderness, forest, animals, earth, oceans, even the sky, all these belong to our understanding. There is so much to understand. And, gentlemen, there is a dominion to assert.

Halley *is now dressed and ready. He is in Greenwich. Lights change to . . .*

Scene Seven

Halley *at Greenwich buoyantly surveying what is now his observatory.* **Anstey** *on, looks older, damaged.*

Halley Oh, the years have dropped away. Only 64. I can feel the energy surge. An entirely new observatory just there – a dome that will facilitate accurate observation under civilised conditions. Three assistants working simultaneously. Observations on all the cometary activity in the universe as far as the telescopes can see. I can't wait to get my hands on them.

Anstey I need to rest.

Halley I've earned this, Philip, waited years for it. (*Chuckle.*) Good old Flamsteed, precise to the last. Dying in the last hour of the last day of the year.

Anstey I won't go up to the house.

Halley No, I don't suppose you will. Oh, an observatory of my own at last. Oh . . . (*Beat.*) The clocks are the best in the world you know. Perfect. Matched Thomas Tompians, built for simultaneous correction. Worth thousands.

Mrs Flamsteed *approaches.*

Mrs Flamsteed Value is a matter of buying or selling, Doctor Halley. Sir Philip.

Anstey Madam.

Mrs Flamsteed Not opinion. Value must be tested in the market place.

Halley Madam. Please accept my most sincere condolences on this tragic loss. Though comfort yourself with the knowledge that it is not only your loss but that of the entire scientific community. His book will be his monument. Do you have his book somewhere to hand? Let me relieve you of the worry.

Mrs Flamsteed You are an old man in an unseemly hurry.

Halley The Royal Society has empowered me, your husband's friend, to –

Mrs Flamsteed Friend? His last reference to you was, I quote: 'Halley, the lapdog that licks Newton's . . .' the precise anatomical detail escapes me.

Halley (*pause*) Please be so good as to examine this inventory of the instruments believed to be here. They are the property of The Royal Society.

Mrs Flamsteed *examines the list.*

Mrs Flamsteed Oh, there's much more than this.

Halley More? I'll take them in hand . . . at your convenience.

Mrs Flamsteed Or was, it's all gone now.

Halley Gone?

Mrs Flamstecd Sold off. But he said to keep you a box. The key.

Halley *takes key and looks at a piece of paper she gives him.*

Halley What is it?

Mrs Flamsteed An insult, I imagine. I wish to be faithful to his memory in some respects at least.

Halley Those instruments were –

Mrs Flamsteed My property. Legally and morally.

Hands him a document.

As you see. I earned them.

Halley The catalogue?

Mrs Flamsteed Arrangements have been made for publication. It appears to have some commercial value, God knows why.

Halley Those were astronomical clocks.

Mrs Flamsteed Well, I got an astronomical price for them.

Halley How much?

Mrs Flamsteed Ask the new owner.

Halley You don't know what you are destroying.

Mrs Flamsteed I do.

Halley Vandalism. I will dispute this.

Mrs Flamsteed You'll lose in the courts and look a great fool everywhere else. And you're too old to waste the energy. I am quite determined, there is a future to finance.

Halley Do I have your permission to inspect the house, there is I hope, no question of ownership.

Mrs Flamsteed Just common decency.

Halley *goes.*

Two years.

Anstey Two years.

Mrs Flamsteed And Africa?

Anstey Never got past the Canaries. Picked a little something up. He always said Africa would find me out. Well it didn't. You find yourself out. In the end.

Mrs Flamsteed What are you then?

Anstey Dead. (*Laughs.*) As dead as the stars. And reason, I am afraid, offers little comfort. (*Beat.*) Margaret –

Mrs Flamsteed Is one supposed to care? (*Pause.*) Really?

Halley *on.*

Halley This is disgraceful. The house is stripped bare, the entire house! As if . . .

Mrs Flamsteed He had never lived. That house was my prison. It's yours now. We shall be gone by the end of the week.

Anstey We?

Mrs Flamsteed My daughter and I.

Anstey (*pause*) Doctor Halley. Doctor Halley!

Halley *finally takes the hint and goes.*

Mrs Flamsteed She is in the park with the nurse.

Anstey Mine?

Mrs Flamsteed No. Mine.

Anstey (*pause*) No words. Don't know what to say. (*Shivers.*) My mother . . . my mother says that men . . . are afraid . . . that is the great secret. See it, she says, in the eyes. (*Beat.*) A girl?

Mrs Flamsteed Yes. A girl. Sir Philip, you are a man of the world, you have had a career, answer me this: what future for a girl? Lizzie? The girl who put you to bed? Me? And all the others, all of them, all those countless little creatures, numerous as the stars. You fucked us all.

Anstey Ah. Such intemperate language. But look at me now. I'm reformed, from libertine to scientist.

Mrs Flamsteed Merely . . . a shift of emphasis.

Anstey (*beat*) Cold up here. This winter chill.

Halley *on.*

Halley Philip? There's much to do. I will have my own instruments transported tomorrow. (*Looks up, then around.*) See for miles. On this hill we are above the world.

Anstey Well, if a man can't be a human being at least he can be a god.

Mrs Flamsteed No future in that.

Anstey No future? (*Pause.*) So?

Mrs Flamsteed So. As I said . . .

She looks out too, shades her eyes against the sun.

Mine.

Mrs Flamsteed *walks down towards the child.* **Anstey** *and* **Halley** *are left in possession.*

Beached

Beached was first performed at the Croydon Warehouse on 5 March 1987, with the following cast.

Pete	Ian Target
Maria	Leonie Mellinger

Directed by Celia Bannerman
Designed by Michael Pavelka
Lighting by John A Williams

The play was revived at the Old Red Lion, Islington on 12 June 1990, with the same cast, director and designer. Lighting by Matthew Evered. Assistant Director, Lisa Napier.

Note

Pete is in his late teens, not unattractive. Not terribly clever either. Maria is around 17/18, sharp, small, streetwise.

Act One

Scene One

Downstage: A sandy beach strewn with litter. An old oil drum buried in the sand. Upstage: A high concrete wall with a metal ladder. Set into it, the mouth of a huge outflow pipe covered with metallic mesh. A low ledge under this.

Night. Darkness. A red light glow in the distance. We hear the sea close by. **Pete** *on with rucksack, carrying a sleeping bag and wrapped within it a cashbox. He crosses to the wall, climbs it, stops at the top, listens.*

Pete Maria? Can you 'ear it?

Pete *drops over the wall.* **Maria** *on, carrying an old sports bag. She has been dragging after* **Pete** *for miles. They are both exhausted.*

Maria Then I 'ad this job, winder dressin'.

She crosses to ladder, talking to **Pete** *over wall.*

Pete (*off*) What?

Maria I was in the window. I look up and this feller 'as it out. Broad daylight. In the street. It was standin' there like a rat with a cold, sniffin'. And then it snots. All down the glass . . . These shoes is bleedin useless . . . Eight in the mornin' polishin' winders so wankers got a good view. Fuck that. Get another job servin' on – tapas. And then I pack that in 'cause of somethin'. And then this fella I'm livin' with – (*Beat.*) Well, long and short is 'Buona Sera Papa'. An' he stares at me, mouth open, this wet cod in his hand drippin' batter all down his trousers. The customers go quiet. (*Pause.*) And then 'e says 'You come back to Papa?' (*Pause.*) And then 'e gives it me: first the cod, an' then the slags an' cunts an' . . .

Pete *appears over wall.* **Maria** *stares.*

Your teeth are chatterin'. Never seen that before.

Pete (*shivers*) Where's the duvet?

Maria I dunno.

Pete You 'ad it.

Maria No!

Pete I give it to you. Sure I did. (*Pause:*) Could be anywhere.

Maria Better look for it then.

Pete *does not move.*

Maria Go on then. Look.

Pete Where?

Maria Where we been.

Pete *looks round in confusion.*

Pete But where 'ave we been?

Maria Don' ask me, I been followin' you.

Pete We're lost then?

Maria Yeah.

Pete Oh . . . we're fuckin' lost.

Maria Looks like it.

Pete Fuckin' hell.

Maria Who's fault's that?

Pete Typical, innit? I mean, bleedin', fuckin' typical.

Maria Is it?

Pete What d'you think? (*To himself.*) No! C'mon, Peter, calm yourself down. This is the place. This has got to be the place. Same road. Same path. This pipe. (*Points.*) Power station.

Maria You all right?

Pete Things look different in the dark. And this mist.

Abruptly rushes almost off. Stops, turns.

Just, don't move.

Puts down rucksack, and keeping hold of the cashbox, starts to go.

Maria You goin' now?

Pete Don't move, all right?

Pete *goes to look for duvet with cashbox.*

Maria All right.

Maria *rubs her cold feet.*

Peter?

Jumps to her feet and hops from foot to foot.

Oh, these shoes is bleedin' useless.

Sits down and takes out a book, reads it by torchlight.

Ecco. Ecco . . . 'Where you been?' – Nowhere – 'Where you been?', 'little cunt', 'fuckin' whore'. (*Pause.*) Learned really good English did my dad.

Pete (*off*) I can't find it.

Maria (*reading*) Use the torch.

Pete (*off*) You got that.

Maria Oh yeah.

Continues reading, but her thoughts catch up with her.

Eyetie bantam cock. The Mussolini of Catford. Struttin' that swagger arse all the way from the pickled onions in their jar to the chicken on 'is rotisserie.

Pete (*off*) I found it. It's all right. It's dry.

Maria Eileen. (*Sings.*) 'O sole mio!' (*Mimics giggling.*) 'Was it you in the circus when you was in Italy, Mr Pioli?' 'O solo mio.' 'Are you sure you wasn't in the circus when you was in Italy, Mr Pioli?' Where do these people get their ideas from?

Maria *gets up and walks restlessly as she talks.*

What you doin'? 'O solo – ' it's all 'e knows, first three words. Slow and sly and very, very thick, Eileen, all made up. Tarty . . . sickly like . . . somethin' left over in the cake shop winder for a very long time – and even the flies won't shit on it no more. But Giovanni? 'E was *impressed*.

Pete *returns with the duvet. Still clutching the cashbox.*

Pete Look, I found it. (*Beat.*) What you readin' in the dark for?

Maria I want to learn Italian.

Pete In the dark?

Maria Don't want to waste no time. People expect Eyeties speak Italian.

Pete Look, dry. It was only just down there. You must have dropped it.

Maria Where are we? What is this place?

Pete Bird sanctuary. All the way back, it's a safe place for them to be.

Pete *comes over to* **Maria**.

There's a kind of goose.

Maria Goose?

Pete Only place it comes in the whole of England is here. You ever seen 'em fly?

Maria I seen swans.

Pete Fly though?

Maria No, their wings was clipped.

Pete Way they lift off . . . like there was no force to keep 'em down.

Maria Where you seen that?

Pete Here.

Maria So, you been here before then?

Pete How d'you think I found the way?

Maria And now you come back?

Pete It's dangerous that marsh, people get lost in it, die and things. Come down on a school trip when I was a kid to see the power station, but I run off and found it. (*Gestures along the beach.*) There's no people you know, not for miles, the marsh keeps them off. (*Beat.*) Just me and the birds. Fuckin' marvellous. Come again on me own. Got all these maps and everything. It was the same. Sat there and just looked at it – all day. Sand . . . sea . . . sun. It's my place, Maria. I know I can rely on it.

Maria Couldn't you pick on somewhere warmer?

Pete We'll be all right there.

Maria What you on about?

Pete On our own. (*Beat.*) My place. Just a bit further.

Maria We been travellin' all night.

Pete Nearly there, the exact place I found.

Maria This'll do. I'm tired. And you're lost.

Pete I know, I know exactly where I'm going. Exactly.

He looks around uncertainly.

Maria I can't even remember my mother.

Pete Who?

Maria Me mother . . .

Pete What. (*Beat.*) You was little.

Maria My mother.

Pete *climbs a dune.*

Pete Mist's clearing – look, the lights.

Maria His sister done all that for him. Aunt Gina! She was the nearest I had. Your husband, your husband got to be absolutely sure about your . . . hymen, or he go on and on and on for ever. Take my word for it: Tampax – no good. (*To* **Pete**.) Where we going?

Pete This way.

Maria 'Your mother,' she says, 'your real mother is dead'. And every time she says it . . . (*To* **Pete**.) Where we going? Can't keep me eyes open.

Pete We got to go this way. Power station.

Maria What's them lights?

Pete Power station . . . like I told ya. Smell that salt. 'S like Margate.

Maria Cold enough. You gone and got us lost, ain't ya?

Pete *makes his way over to the wall, dazed, trying to take his bearings in the darkness. The torchbeam stabs out into the darkness.*

Pete I know exactly. Power station. Over there. And my beach . . . there's a bit of a drop, and then the sea comes round again on the other side, over there. So we go along here a bit further and we can climb down.

Pete *starts to climb ladder again.*

Maria Do we have to?

Pete We'll be safe then. (*Pauses on the top of the wall.*) Gawd, smell that sea.

Maria *stands.*

Maria I got sand in me shoes.

Pete Listen. (*Pause.*) It's like in one of them shells.

Maria What?

Pete *plays his torch over the sea.*

Pete Waves. On the beach.

Maria Then why can't I see them?

Pete You can 'ear them, can't ya? Waves breakin' for miles and miles, all along the beach.

Maria I'm tired. I want to sleep.

Pete *drops over the wall.* **Maria** *starts to climb the ladder.*

Pete (*off*) Nearly there. C'mon.

Maria Which way?

Pete (*off*) There.

She slips, falls back onto to the beach.

(*Off.*) Maria?

Silence.

(*Off.*) Where are ya? (*Pause.*) Where you gone?

Pete *at top again.*

You all right?

He finds her in the torchlight.

Maria (*winded*) You . . . prong. You useless . . . dick'eaded . . . fuckin' prong.

Pete Don't move.

Maria (*groans*) Move?

Pete Don't move nothin'.

He scrambles down.

You int 'urt yourself?

Maria *cries.*

Pete You int broke nothin'?

Maria (*cries*) My arm 'urts.

Pete Let's see.

Pete *rushes over to* **Maria**.

Maria No.

Pete Come on.

Maria Me arm!

Pete It's broken, it's fuckin' broken. Oh Jesus Christ, please, no. Don't let it be broken.

Maria It 'urts.

Pete Bend it. (*He looks at her arm.*)

Maria Be careful.

Pete It's all right if you can bend it. (*He moves her arm.*) Thank Gawd for that.

Pete *almost faints with relief.*

Maria Knocked the breath right out of me. You don't care, do ya? My side. It's hurtin'.

Pete Where?

Lifts up her top. Silently feels for broken bones.

Maria Your fingers is ice.

Pete (*pause*) I can feel your ribs.

Maria (*pause*) Just ribs.

Pete You're little, ain't ya, really?

Maria (*pause*) Just ribs, that's all.

Pete I can feel your 'eart. Found this bird once, cats had got to it and broke its wing. (*Pause.*) I could feel its 'eart beatin'.

Maria Yeah?

Pete Can I . . . touch you?

Maria You're touching me.

Pete I mean . . . somewhere else.

Maria Your 'ands'll be cold.

Pete Outside.

Maria What?

Pete On the outside of your clothes – I'll be careful.

Maria I'm not glass.

He touches her breast. Silence.

Pete Christ.

Maria It's freezin'.

Pete Jesus Christ.

Maria I'm freezin'.

Pete Just perfect.

Maria What happened to the bird?

Pete Hopeless, weren't it?

Maria Where's the bags?

Pete *looks round for his rucksack.* **Maria** *looks along the beach.*

Let's get warm, eh? (*Beat.*) Where's the light gone?

Pete Dunno . . . must be the mist.

Maria Dark enough. Can't see your 'and in front of your face.

Pete *comes back with stuff, gives* **Maria** *the duvet. She lays it out. She lights a cigarette.*

Pete 'Ere.

Maria Ta.

Pete Listen –

Maria I 'ate the dark.

Pete – nothin'. We're safe. (*Lights cigarette.*) Look at that. Miles and miles of it all the way round the earth. I like the dark, always 'ave.

Pete *discovers that* **Maria** *has set up on her own. He lays out the sleeping bag on the other side of the rucksack.* **Maria** *puts out her cigarette and lies down.*

Used to get in the corner under my bed for hours, with the cat, and nobody'd know I was there. Dark does somethin' to the sound – the walls was thin in our house. That school trip . . .

Maria I'm tired. (*Grunts.*) Mmm . . .

Pete *gets into the sleeping bag, leans out and unpacks rucksack, coffee mugs out, water in an old lemonade bottle, camping stove.*

Pete That power station, this big building and these engine things, fuckin' enormous. These . . . things big as buses and vibratin'. (*Pause.*) No, not 'avin' that, I thought. So I fucked off. Turned round and fucked off. I went straight through the door, through the gate, and this fat ol' cunt of a teacher come runnin' after. 'Where you going?' he goes. 'Where d'you think you're goin'?' Used to play for Millwall or somethin', 'e did. Years ago, though – 'cos I left 'im on 'is 'ands and knees in the sand coughin' 'is lungs out. No chance. 'I'll 'ave you for this,' he goes, but I just ran and ran. Till I come 'ere. (*Beat.*) And then I stopped. (*Pause.*) Me 'ands is shakin'. Look at 'em. Maria?

Maria *is asleep.*

I wouldn't go back for nothing. I was scared shitless. 'I'll 'ave you for this.' (*Pause.*) And 'e did. (*He picks up cashbox.*) They always do if you go back. (*Pause.*) Oh fuck, the key! I forgot the key!

Pete *puts out torch.*

Blackout.

Scene Two

Beach, morning. **Maria** *and* **Pete** *are asleep.* **Maria** *stirs under the duvet.*

Maria (*looking out*) Bleedin' 'ell.

She wraps herself up like a caterpillar, crawls over to the bag and examines the butane stove, the pan, the water bottle and finally the flask.

'Urry up. Ain't natural sleep like that 'ere. (*Shouts.*) We're still 'ere.

Pete Wha'?

Maria Hello.

Pete Wha'?

Maria The rest of us. Me and the rest of the world. We're out here waitin' for ya.

Pete Wha'?

Maria You might be missin' somethin' good in there.

Pete (*sits*) Fuckin' 'ell.

Maria Bad, innit?

Pete What's this?

Maria Well bad! (*Grins.*) Watch.

She does a caterpillar mime in her duvet.

Caterpillar. An' then . . . butterfly! (*She crawls up to him, touches his shoulder.*) Cold, see. (*Touches his face.*) Coffee's on. It's all 'appened, Peter, just like you 'ope it 'asn't. Everything. You may 'ave been dreamin' it away in there, but out 'ere it all counts.

Maria *takes lid off flask.* **Pete** *rubs his eyes.*

Pete There was more seagulls.

Maria Yeah?

Pete Where they gone?

Maria Cuddled up in their nests with their mums. What's 'appening, then?

Pete Tide's gone out. You askin' me?

Maria You brung us 'ere.

Pete But –

Maria Wasn't my idea, come 'ere.

Pete We 'ad to 'ave somewhere to go.

Maria Let's go there then.

Pete We better do something.

Maria Well?

Pete Build a fire or something.

Maria Why?

Pete Is that coffee?

Maria *starts to make coffee.*

Maria It's cold. I ain't stayin' 'ere, Peter, not really.

Pete There'll be wood further down.

Maria 'Ow about Manchester?

Pete We can use it to build a fire.

Maria Newcastle, Glasgow . . .

Hands coffee to **Pete**, *keeps her own.*

Pete (*looks around*) Must be further down. (*Pause.*) I don't know nothing about them places.

Maria Neither do I.

Pete I don't even know how to get there.

Maria We'll find out. You fancy me then?

Pete (*Beat.*) There's wood all over these beaches.

Maria 'Course you do.

Pete It falls off the ships of its own accord.

Maria Last night . . . You remember? (*Pause.*) You think I'm pretty.

Pete Didn't think it'd be this cold.

Maria You get the sleeping bag.

Pete The quilt's the best thing.

Maria Me feet stick out.

Pete Where?

Maria *shows her feet.*

Maria Lurin' me down 'ere without a proper sleepin' bag.

Pete I only brung the one.

Maria Why not buy two?

Pete Buy it! I nicked it, didn't I?

Maria What, all of it? (*She indicates the kit.*)

Pete Yeah.

Maria Where?

Pete Here an' there.

Maria You 'ave been planning.

Pete Lots of stuff round, if you keep your eyes open.

Maria Where d'you get it all?

Pete Oh, 'ere and there. You know that big house on the corner where all them students used to live?

Maria Yeah?

Pete (*holds up sleeping bag*) They left it out on the line. Deserve everything they get. (*He points out various bits of gear.*) Woollys. Halfords. Asda.

Maria I didn't know you did that.

Pete Don't do it all the time. Just for here. I had this plan, a sort of . . . holiday, thought I'd come down here in the summer and give me mother a break. She in't well. And she wants to be on her own. (*Pause.*) So I been savin' things up for a bit of the old campin', always fancied it.

Maria Why's she want to be on her own when she's ill?

Pete I dunno, do I? (*Pause.*) Says she wants to think things over. (*Pause.*) All she ever fuckin' does is think things over, all fuckin' day long. (*Pause.*) She don't have to lift a finger, not a finger, I do everything – cleanin', shoppin', food, everything. All she has to do is sit there 'an think things over. (*Pause.*) When I found out she was ill I thought . . . I thought maybe she would . . . but she turns round and says, out of nowhere she says, 'Peter, piss off.'

Maria *smothers a giggle.*

It ain't funny. Not when it's yourself. Ain't funny then. (*Pause.*) So I been lookin' round . . . for something else.

Maria And here I am. Let's in.

Maria *gets into* **Pete***'s sleeping bag.*

Pete What you –

Maria C'mon.

Pete I . . .

Maria Whass the matter? C'mon!

Pete I ain't . . . got . . .

Maria Let's in, I'm freezin' out 'ere.

Pete I ain't got no . . .

Maria (*grins*) No, you 'aven't, 'ave you?

Pete *picks up mug.*

Pete I can't help it. I said, didn't I?

Maria Well, no.

Pete I did, I said.

Maria 'S only natural.

Pete I said, I hadn't got none on.

Pete *drinks. Long pause.*

Maria 'S warmin' up in 'ere innit? They do this when they rescue people on mountains. Somebody I used to know told me all about it, he used to climb mountains an' all that sort of thing. Did you know that a human being gives out as much energy as a 100 watt light bulb?

Pete Yeah?

Maria Yeah. He told me that. He was a student. Gone now though. Why d'you pick on this place?

Pete Everybody needs somewhere to go.

Maria 'Ope it ain't thinkin' of snowin'.

Pete (*looks at the sky*) It's spring – officially.

Maria 'E swept me off me feet in the Washeteria. I think it was my dirty washin' turned him on. He had this thing about sweaty bras, don't ask me why.

She kisses him.

Pete I ain't 'ad a wash or nuffin'.

Maria Neither 'ave I.

Pete I mean, since before we left. I was in an 'urry. I didn't think it would . . . come up, you know?

Maria 'S all right.

Pete I'm clean though. I wash regular, mornin' an' evenin'. Every day.

Maria Plenty of water out there.

Pete I ain't goin' in that.

Maria No . . .

Pete Kill meself.

Confused pause.

Maria That's why I come in 'ere with you, get warmed up. It's more friendly.

Pete We 'ad this kid at school never washed. Smelled of piss all the time. Got sent 'ome for it one day. I'm not like that.

Maria No.

Pete His clothes was stiff with dirt. (*Pause.*) Tramp. (*Pause.*) Least I was clean.

She holds his penis inside the sleeping bag.

Maria What's this then?

Pete (*pause*) Your 'ands are freezin'.

Maria It's your own fault for takin' your trousers off.

Pete I always take me trousers off in bed.

Maria You been like this before?

Pete No. You?

Maria Oh yeah, lots of times.

Pete 'Ave you?

Maria What d'you think?

Pete That student?

Maria Prat. 'E 'ad this old gramophone, wind-up thing, an' these stupid old records nobody's ever 'eard of he got in the junk shop on the Lee High Road. Played 'em for hours, lyin' there an' staring at the ceiling, playin' these records and smokin' – you know – hours and hours. (*Pause.*) Mad. 'E was the one I run off with. Pazzo.

Pete I didn't know that.

Maria No?

Pete I never knew you went off *with* somebody.

Maria Didn't you guess?

Pete No, I didn't.

Maria Well, this is it, Peter. I'm with you now. And this is what you come for. It's all right, you don't 'ave to pretend or nothin'. (*She rolls on top of him and shuffles around.*) You want to take 'em off?

No answer.

You want me to? I thought you might.

No answer.

All right.

She wriggles out of her pants.

Talkative, ain't ya?

She gets into position.

I'm protected if that's it . . . on the pill an' that. Go on then.

Pause.

You . . . You . . . worried, are you? Are you?

No answer.

Pete I . . .

Maria Yeah?

She gets him inside her.

All you got to do is move. Just . . . listen, I *know* you want to don't I? 'S obvious. Go on. I can *feel* you inside me. Go on! Chrissakes!

Pause.

Please.

Pause.

Look, it 'as to be *you*. Move, will ya?

Pete I can't.

Maria I can *feel* that you can.

Pete I can't!

Maria Why not?

Pete I keep seein' 'im lying there.

Maria Peter . . .

Pete Please.

Maria Pete –

He struggles to get away from her.

Why not?

Pete Leave me alone.

Pause.

Maria What's wrong? What's wrong with me?

He drags himself out of the sleeping bag.

Look out Pete, you're 'urtin'! You're 'urtin' me!

Maria *has ended up curled up in the sleeping bag, sobbing quietly.*

Pete I was standin' there, Maria, and 'e saw, right, he saw straight through me. The smile creepin' all over 'is face. Joke, eh? Me nickin' 'is money, what a laugh. (*Pause.*) I didn't mean it. It was an accident.

They both dress in silence.

Scene Three

Maria *tries to light stove.* **Pete** *faces stage.*

Pete You didn't even ask what 'ad 'appened?

Maria I know.

Pete And 'e's your father.

Maria I know that an' all.

Pete They gonna fuckin' kill me for what I done to 'im.

Maria Him? You done 'im a favour.

Pete 'Cept they ain't gonna get me. I ain't goin' back, no fuckin' way!

Maria Nice bandage round 'is 'ead, Eileen givin' 'im the tit every 'alf hour. 'E'll be all right.

Pete *examines driftwood.*

Pete There was lots of things when I come 'ere before. All the way down, for miles.

Maria *examines the stove.*

Maria Won't turn.

Pete Wood an' everything.

Maria It's rusty, won't turn.

Pete No.

Maria Where you been keepin' it?

Pete In the shed.

Maria In the wet?

Pete Maybe things only come up from the ships in the summer and that's why. Maybe it's tides or something.

Maria Peter . . .

Maria *gives up with trying to make the stove work and opens a tin of pineapple chunks.*

Pete I must 'ave 'it 'im really 'ard you know, 'cause . . .'cause 'e was flying straight across the room. Hit the wall an' 'ung there. Like that cat does in them cartoons on the telly. An' then 'e slid down.

Maria Like the cat?

Pete Yeah. Sat down. And then this blood out of 'is nose. I couldn't believe it. (*Pause.*) I 'aven't even looked properly, 'ave I? We could build a camp.

Maria What?

Pete There was lots of good stuff before, just right. I remember standin' 'ere and thinkin', just right for a camp.

Maria To live in?

Pete For a bit. (*Looks around.*) Plastic bottles, 'undreds of them:

Harpic, an' Domestos, and Sainsbury's an' everything. They
never rot, you know. Go round and round the world for ever.

Maria Live 'ere?

Pete Just for a bit.

Maria You get Robinson Crusoe out the library, then? Pazzo!

Pete I don't understand that.

Pete *paces beach restlessly.*

Maria Mad! Live 'ere!

Maria *takes out 'Teach Yourself Italian'.*

Pete Where else is there?

Maria Off your bleedin' 'ead.

Pete We can't go back.

Maria Well, I ain't stayin' 'ere.

Maria *opens her book.*

Pete Maria . . .

Maria No chance.

Pete You don't understand what I done.

Maria No?

Pete He 'ad a knife in his 'and, didn't 'e? He was goin' to stick
me with it, wasn't 'e? I 'ad to do somethin', didn't I? (*Pause.*) I
didn't mean to 'urt 'im.

Maria Credo di dover . . .

Pete What?

Maria . . . andare. (*Explains.*) Nearest I can get. Credo di dover
andare. I think I'll have to go, Peter.

Pete But where?

Maria Any fuckin' where.

Pete (*pause*) He'll be all right though, no need to worry.

Maria 'Bout 'im?

Pete What d'you think?

Maria (*pause. She faces* **Pete**) I'll tell you a story, shall I? 'Bout when I was younger. Thirteen. And 'im, on 'is own with me. Me growin' up, 'im wonderin' 'ow I'm goin' to turn out. Well . . . every time 'e goes down the pub, 'e locks me in. With me chocolate and me crisps and the portable telly. And at first I can't work it out: And then it dawns. (*Pause.*) What 'e thinks is, first fella I see – I'm on me back with me legs wide open, waitin' for it. That's what 'e thinks.

Pete So 'e locks you in.

Maria I don't like that. I ain't 'avin' that. So . . . one night, one Monday night I'm out the winder and leggin' it down Lewisham with some of the naughty girls from school. Disco. (*Pause.*) I mean, what did I expect, eh? Moonlight in me Chianti? Candlelight on me chips? Well, what I got was warm lager, lots and lots of warm lager, and these three fellas, this band, in the back of their van . . . one after the other.

Silence.

Didn't know what was 'appenin'. Thirteen and pissed, see. (*Pause.*) Long walk 'ome, I tell ya. (*Pause.*) But . . . by the time 'e's openin' the front door there I am, tucked up in bed, all safe and sound. With this 'andful of J-Cloths and ice between my legs. And prayin', oh sweet Maria, prayin' I can 'old off cryin' long enough, 'cause every particle tells me if 'e finds out, 'e's goin' to kill me, I mean really kill me. But it's *all right*. Door opens. 'Buona notte, Mariucca'. Papa . . . and I almost cry, I almost . . . the thing that saves me is the smell on 'im, beer. That smell. Them fellas. 'Im. (*Pause.*) That was the last of 'im for me. No, Peter, I ain't worried about Giovanni.

Maria *goes to her bag – searches for and finds purse.*

You 'urt me.

Pete I didn't mean . . . I couldn't (*Beat.*) 'elp meself.

Maria Everybody thinks they can do what they like, just what they like, just what they fuckin' like.

Pete Maria . . .

Maria Leave me alone.

Pete (*pause*) What you going to do?

Maria Go back.

Pete You can't, they'll be waitin'. In the shop.

Maria Somewhere else then, Maida Vale, I been there before. I can 'andle that.

Maria *puts purse in her pocket.*

Pete They got your name. They got it all down, on computers, everything.

Maria I done it before.

Pete That was different. It's safe 'ere.

Maria Cold. Damp. Nothing. (*She cradles her arm.*) You 'urt me.

Pete 'E was standin' there with this knife, 'e was goin' to say something.

Maria Like what? 'I cutta it off'?

Pete Listen!

Maria 'Vendette, Pietro!' He's fuckin' mad, Giovanni, know that? Oh yes – seen 'The Godfather' seven times, sittin' there in the dark, thumbin' the blade of 'is fillettin' knife. Nobody's safe. He 'eard a noise upstairs. Course 'e 'ad a knife in 'is 'and.

Pete He smiled at me.

Maria He was relieved.

Pete They'll be lookin' right now.

Maria What do they care?

Pete They'll care about 'im, 'cos of the shop, 'cos of the money.

Maria Once round the Rose and Whatsit see if the fivers smell of skate an' that's that.

Pete (*pause*) Looked real bad lyin' there.

Maria (*indifferent*) Yeah?

Pete It's all right for you.

Maria What?

Pete Way 'e treated you, your face, they'll understand that. Who's going to understand me though, eh? They don't know nothin' 'bout me.

Maria What is there to know?

Pete 'Im. 'Im and that *whore*.

Maria Eileen?

Pete No. All they'll care 'bout is what I done. Nothin' else.

Pete *walks away.* **Maria** *follows quickly.*

Maria What whore?

Pete *looks out over the beach, chews fingernails.*

Pete (*pause*) Don't matter.

Maria Yes it does.

Pete Forget it, will ya?

Maria Forget what?

Pete (*avoiding*) Where's the driftwood gone? All the way down it was, from right over there, right down there.

Maria *picks up the cashbox and fiddles with it.*

Pete (*turning to watch*) There's no key. (*Their eyes meet.*) I was in an 'urry. I forgot. (*Pause.*) Yeah, I know.

Pete *gets a stone.*

Maria Open it.

Pete *hits the cashbox with the stone.* **Maria** *stands above.*

Pete Maria . . . look, I can't 'elp it right now, way things are. I need some time, right?

Maria Open it.

Another stone.

Pete I ain't never 'it nobody before. Not like that. Christ!

Maria I wish you'd stop bitin' your nails.

Maria *walks off and gets a stone.*

It's horrible.

Pete Look . . . I mean, you and me. I was unprepared . . .

Maria You was ready.

Pete First time, Maria. First time.

Maria You was good and bleedin' ready, know what I mean? All you 'ad to do was move.

Maria *comes to the cashbox.*

Pete I couldn't get 'im out of –

She smashes a stone onto the cashbox.

Maria Move! Not think! (*Pause.*) Oh, Peter, it won't come no easier than that, I tell ya. Oh . . . Only fair . . . I thought . . . you see? That's what he done it for after all, me. For me. The insult – you, turnin' me down. *You!*

Pete There's no wood. (*Lets sand drain through his fingers.*) It looks different in the summer. (*He shows her.*) The sand.

Maria Fuckin' insult of it.

Pete In the sun. Looks yellow then. Walk along, right? And there's things all over – seaweed and crabs. (*Thinks.*) And starfish. Lots of them. Amazin' . . . so beautiful. And birds, hundreds of birds, the sky's full of them. All over. All kinds. In the waves and everywhere. You've got to see it the way it really is, Maria. The way it could be if you just give it a bit of time.

Maria It's winter. Right here, right now, it's winter.

She gets up.

Pete I've seen it different.

Maria (*she sits by wall*) *You* say.

Pete I have, I promise you. Maria . . . (*Sits on barrel.*) Can't stay like this. Let's . . . do somethin'. Somethin' different. Get somethin' started.

Pete *stares out at the sea.* **Maria** *starts to read her book. Silence*

Them ships is goin'.

Maria *looks out to sea.*

'Ardly see them now. (*Pause.*) Gone.

Maria (*softly*) It's the fog.

Pete We 'ave to get warm. Shelter.

Maria I ain't changin' my mind.

Pete Just for now. Keep us warm for now.

Maria I ain't stayin'. My arm's been 'urtin' all this time and I ain't said nothin'.

Pete *gets up and goes over to ladder.*

Pete Mebbe there's some better stuff round the other side. I'll go and see, yeah?

Pete *climbs the ladder and goes.* **Maria** *takes out the purse. Looks at box and speaks.*

Maria I got this letter from 'er. Just the one. Christ only knows, even that must 'ave been 'ard enough after all them years. Tiny writin' and a red stamp, some kind of leaf with the Queen's 'ead in the corner. Canada. I held it. I'd been waitin' so long, you see, I wanted . . . take me time. But suddenly he's got it on the fire, the flame's burnin' through and 'is arms is tight round me shoulders. All I can do is watch. That tiny writin'. Her picture curlin' up and burstin' into flame. By then I was cryin', we was both cryin'. Watched it burn away till it was delicate black ash spread out like butterfly wings, only black. Then 'e let me go.

When 'e'd gone I tried to pick it up. But it was no use, it just fell apart in me 'ands. All I got was dust.

Maria *goes to box and lifts it. Returns to sit with it on her knee. She takes out the key from her purse.*

Even the photo. (*Beat.*) Fuckin' bastard. I'd never once seen your picture, your face. He'd wiped you out. (*Pause.*) And then I thought – weddin' photos. He'd keep them. Somewhere secret, safe. Please . . .

Maria *opens the box with the key and lays out the contents – bundles of banknotes and, finally, a long buff envelope.*

Please.

She opens it and finds no photograph. We see her extreme disappointment and her recovery, all in silence.

(*Quietly.*) Bastard.

She opens out the document and reads. It is in Italian.

Giovanni . . . Giovanni Pioli . . . Sposo. Sposo?

She looks up the word in 'Teach Yourself Italian'.

It's their weddin' certificate.

She examines it again, more eagerly.

Francesca. Francesca Madrianni.

Act Two

Maria *reading the certificate and eating apple.* **Pete** *dumps beach litter, mainly wood over the wall.* **Maria** *closes the cashbox.*

Pete *climbs over. Pulls out a length of rope.*

Pete Look at this. I knew I was right. See that. It's really strong this old stuff, they used to tar it, last for years. See? Used to flog people with rope like this, 'undreds of lashes till their backs was raw.

Maria *(stands, begins to walk up and down)* Eighteen years old.

Pete I got everything I need now. Give us an 'and. *(To self.)* Everything. *(To her.)* Nails and everything. We can use them.

Maria Real old-fashioned place. They do things in real old-fashioned ways.

Pete Where?

Maria Italy. Naples.

Pete *(looking up)* What's that?

Maria Wedding certificate.

Pete I thought you said you didn't –

Maria Her photo – that's what I said. *(Reads.)* Francesca . . . sun goin' down, girls in pretty dresses, men standin' round and . . . Francesca.

Pete Look. Nails.

Maria *(stares)* What for?

Pete Build a camp.

Shyly he produces a hammer from the rucksack and begins to look over the large collection of pieces of wood.

Got to 'ave a frame that can take the wind. *(Starts to build. Pause.)*

Strong, right? These big bits, 'ere, (*Builds.*) they go together. That's what the nails is for . . . (*Lays more wood out.*) . . . hold them together.

Pete *now works on his frame.*

Always wanted to do this . . . when I was little. Read these books about kids livin' in camps. By the sea. On the beach.

More building of frame.

Maria (*quietly*) Fuckin' 'ell. (*Puts certificate away.*)

Pete Better'n Catford, anyway.

Maria (*looks round*) End of the world.

Pete It's all better'n Catford. I 'ate that fuckin' place. I 'ate every last fuckin' bastard in it. (*Drives pole into sand.*)

Maria What about your mother?

Pete Not one of 'em.

Maria Not even –

Pete Nobody! (**Pete** *sorts out more rope.*) Treat me like shit, all of 'em, all my life, right? (*He ties frame together.*) You know what I am, Maria. So do they, an' there's always this look in their eye. What's 'e know? What's 'e remember? (*Looks up.*) Everything. Yeah, they all been through our back gate one time or another.

Maria Did they?

Pete Yeah, all of 'em. I seen what they're like when they in't pretendin'. 'Eard 'em when they thought nobody was listenin'.

Maria With your mother?

Pete (*ties rope to ladder*) That's what they can't stand, what I know. An' the women is worse. For them I don't even exist, somethin' nasty they don't want to think about. (*Beat.*) Done a lot of readin' when I was little. (*More sorting of rope, then* **Pete** *ties an end of rope from the frame to the ladder, carries on building.*) Always wanted somewhere like this to come to. I could see it in my mind, and when everything was bad – reality an' that – I used to pretend I was there. Inside my mind I was free.

Maria Livin' in your camp?

Pete With you.

Maria Me?

Pete 'Course. You know that. Maria, look at me.

She turns away.

Oh, I looked at you, I looked at you everywhere you went: launderette, papers, grocers, school, everywhere. Used to sit at the window, when I worked in the shop, and wait for you to go up the street. You was always on time. Everywhere you went.

Maria Giovanni liked me regular.

Pete And then one day . . . you disappeared. I was frantic.

Maria *turns away, smiles to herself.*

He told everybody you'd gone to college, get a good education.

Maria *laughs.* **Pete** *gets polythene and puts it over frame.*

'Course nobody believed him. It was obvious you'd just fucked off, but it was like you'd died. They was only streets then without you in them. Dirty and miserable. Months. Then all of a sudden you was back. Only . . . your eye. He'd *marked* you. He'd laid his hands on you. I was so fuckin' *angry*, I could have killed the bastard there and then, could have stuffed that . . . spammy head, that . . . in the boilin' fat and burn it off, boil that dirty, fuckin' pig's face in 'is own fat. He'd hurt you.

Maria 'E made me stand there all night long.

Pete And I made me mind up.

Maria Watchin' them all come in the shop. Face after face. Watchin' their eyes go dead.

Pete I was goin' to look after you.

Maria *looks at him and laughs.*

You love him?

Maria Giovanni?

Pete No, your student. The one you run off with.

Maria What the fuck?

Pete I just wondered . . . if you love him, that's all. I mean . . . I just wondered if 'e was special? (*Pause.*) You seen lots of students then?

Maria (*goes for her pineapple chunks*) What do you mean – how many students, which bits of students, what?

Pete I was just –

Maria Curious?

Pete Was you 'appy?

Maria Yeah, I was 'appy. We 'ad this room in Maida Vale. With this green cover on the bed. Touch of that silk on my skin. Christ. Used to wrap meself in it afterwards and listen to 'im talkin'. 'E thought 'e was educatin' me I think, but I just liked them long words in the sunlight, didn't matter what they meant. Yeah, I was 'appy for a while.

Pete 'E sling you out?

Maria Nosey, in't ya?

Pete What 'appened?

Maria (*walks downstage*) I got to thinkin' about things. And before you ask what, it ain't none of your business. (*Pause.*) Nothin' lasts for ever. Somethin' 'appens, and you get to thinkin' and then everythin' goes wrong.

Pete You love 'im?

Maria I dunno.

Pete 'E love you?

Maria I dunno, do I?

Pause. **Pete** *pulls frame back to the wall.* **Maria** *wanders. They have their backs to each other as* **Pete** *fiddles with his camp, trying not to listen to what she is saying.*

We was at this party once. This big 'ouse full of them. Well
pissed. I'm leanin' against these French winders, right? An' 'e
goes to kiss me, an' all of a sudden there we are, rollin' about on
the grass, laughin' our 'eads off. Winders was open. Fell right
through 'em. (*Beat.*) I can see this big yeller lampshade in the
room, just like the moon . . . so fuckin' like. An' I look down at
what's left of me wine an' it's silver with moonlight . . . I could
'ave sworn. Almost real. We stayed there that night. Didn't need
no clothes at all it was so warm. (*Glances over her shoulder at* **Pete**.)
Summer, you see?

He walks across to the rucksack.

Slept in the greenhouse, it was full of these dark flowers, petals
all over my face like soft little 'ands. It was nice.

Behind her, **Pete** *in his wandering, finds the box and key. He is
shocked.*

Fact, it was very nice.

Pete You cunt.

Maria What?

Pete You 'ad the key all the time.

Maria What d'you call me?

Pete Why d'you make me go through all that if you 'ad the key
all the time? (*Pause.*) Well?

Pete finds the money and pulls it out of the box.

Jesus Christ, look at this!

Maria Cunt.

Pete Just look at it!

Maria That's what you said.

Pete My Gawd. It's too much.

Maria Peter?

Pete They gonna miss it, all this.

Maria When I get called that it makes me think of that van an' them fellas.

She comes up behind him.

Peter, d'you know what it felt like in that van with them fellas?

Pete What you goin' on –

Maria *thrusts her fingers down his throat, almost choking him. He coughs and gasps for breath.*

Maria Like that, cunt.

Pete *suddenly realises the hammer is in his hand.*

Pete C'mon then. C'mon.

They stare at each other, then **Pete** *lets the hammer drop.*

What d'you do that for?

Maria You was gonna 'it me, wasn't ya?

Pete No.

Maria Well you 'it 'im.

Pete That was an accident.

Maria Oh yeah?

Pete *lights a cigarette and paces.* **Maria** *climbs the ladder a few rungs and looks.*

Which way's back?

Pete It's Sunday. Ain't easy, travel on Sundays. No trains. Or buses. Or anything. I ain't just sayin' it.

Maria Which way?

Pete There's nowhere to go.

Maria Yes there is.

Pete Where?

Maria Canada. That's where I'm goin'.

Pete Second biggest country in the world, Canada.

Maria *struggles with stove, making coffee.*

Maria Yeah?

Pete Thousands of miles of frozen wilderness.

Maria She don't live in that.

Pete How d'you know?

Maria She lives in a city, like normal people.

Pete Camp, Canada – same thing.

Maria Same thing? Same thing as you readin' about Robinson Crusoe to keep your mind off what your mother's doin' upstairs.

Pete Ain't funny.

Maria I ain't laughin'. (*Pause.*) Who was it come to see 'er, then?

Pete I told ya. Everybody.

Maria Who though? (*Pause.*) I mean, who exactly? (*Pause.*) Well?

Pete (*reluctantly*) Fella from the minicabs.

Maria Yeah?

Pete Mr French from the Washeteria.

Maria Surprise me. And?

Pete I told ya . . .

Maria You ever see anything?

Pete What?

Maria I bet you 'ave, I bet you seen more dicks than a funeral parlour. (*Pause.*) You must 'ave 'eard things at least.

Pete I didn't listen.

Maria I'd 'ave listened. I'd 'ave made tapes of them. Blackmail the fuckers. So they all come did they?

Pete I don't want to talk about this no more.

Maria Why not?

Pete I just don't.

Maria What she do with you when all this was goin' on? I mean, it must 'ave taken up a lot of 'er time.

Pete Telly. Cartoons an' that. They give me sweets, cheap ones.

Maria Who's your Dad?

Pete I don't know. I was always in the other room when they came.

Maria Not when your father come you wasn't. Who else?

Pete Fuckin' 'ell, I can't remember.

Pete *moves downstage. Kicks stone.*

Maria Can't ya?

Maria *moves off ladder towards* **Pete**.

What's she like, your mother, nice?

Pete (*quietly*) Leave it.

Maria You like her?

She lobs a stone at him.

You can't go back now.

Lobs another stone at him. He swats at it.

She threw you out.

Pete Leave it.

Maria And you got nowhere left to go.

Pete *turns and goes for* **Maria**, *stops himself.*

Oh Peter, that wouldn't be no accident, would it?

Pete I wasn't goin' to do nothin'.

Maria Nowhere, 'ave ya?

Pete No, I 'aven't.

Maria Giovanni –

Pete Fuck off, Maria. Leave me alone.

Pete *makes to go for the box. He stops, looks at her as she stands over it. He goes for it and she snatches a £20 note from the box.*

Maria Look in Giovanni's eyes when he gets one of these. An' 'e does this – every time.

She goes through a routine, showing what Giovanni did with £20 notes, flattening them in the palm of his hand and wiping them on his bum before putting them into the cash register.

Every time. Couldn't stop 'imself. Oh, money. Old-fashioned place like Naples, you can buy yourself a wife. Young girl. Virgin. 'Ow the world melts for ya. (*Pause.*) When 'e's restin' in the shop, right? 'E's got this way of standin' with 'is arms wrapped round the cash register, rubbin' it up and down, up an' down, up an' down. Eileen! All over. Just the same: big brass front with buttons all the way down, glassy eyes with pound note signs in 'em, spring-loaded drawers. It's Eileen! (*Pause.*) Night I come back I 'eard 'em downstairs. 'Im and Eileen. At it. Typical Giovanni, find a way to fuck a cash register.

She crumples the note and throws it aside.

Pete What you doin'?

Maria It's nothing.

Pete It's all crumpled now.

Maria So?

Pete It's money.

Maria I know. I watched 'im earn it. Pound by pound. Listen:

She crouches down and crumples a handful of £20 notes.

Pete Got to be looked after.

Maria Crackles. Like dead leaves.

Pete (*bends down to join her*) There's a fairy story.

Maria You're pathetic, know that?

Pete No, listen. About these children who get lost in the forest. Little girl and little boy. The birds cover them with dead leaves keep them warm. Only the wind blows the leaves away.

Maria *throws down the money, gets up, goes over to ledge and takes a walkman out of her bag. She puts it on loudly.*

Maria No it don't.

Pete Does the way I heard it.

The walkman plays. Another impasse. **Pete** *stubs out his fag and again tries to go for the cash.*

Maria Leave it.

Pete (*pause*) Why?

Maria 'Cause I ask you.

Pete (*pause*) It's not important.

Maria Leave it then.

Pete (*pause*) Wind's gettin' up, it might blow away. (*He stares at the money.*) You know how much that is? You know what I done for it?

Maria (*pulls off walkman*) What was it you done?

Pete *goes for the note but* **Maria** *snatches it out of his hand.*

Pete Maria!

Maria *grabs the box and holds it to* **Pete**'s *groin.*

Maria Tell you what, you put it in 'ere an' I'll wank you some time. Bet you come then.

Pete You . . .

Maria Oh, *finish* it.

Pete You whore.

Maria *puts the box down at* **Pete***'s feet and gets out another £20.*

Maria How many times your mother go down to make one of these? (*Pause.*) Twice?

Pete You cunt.

Maria *starts to circle* **Pete**.

Maria Right. Five times?

Pete You filthy cunt!

Maria Ten times then? Didn't she work cheap!

Pete Cunt!

Maria Was Giovanni there? Was 'e one of them?

Pete Fuckin' cunt.

Maria 'E was, wasn't 'e? Gettin' 'is pound's worth.

He puts the money back in the box.

Pete You know what I did for this? This . . . this mess.

Maria An accident.

Pete You spoiled it!

Maria Was 'e there?

Pete 'Course 'e was there! (*Beat.*) When I was little.

Maria How little?

Pause.

Pete Monday nights.

Maria When I was locked in my room.

Pause.

Maria 'E was with your mother!

Pete My mother's all right!

Maria Your old girl.

Stands.

Pete She's all right.

Maria 'E's down the street fuckin' that cow.

Pete You shut your mouth.

Maria 'S worse than Eileen, this.

Pete I'm warnin' you.

Maria He ain't fit to breathe the same air as my mother. Go with that cow, he'll go with anything.

Pete Least she kept me. Least she didn't piss off with some fella soon as I was born and never once, never once send a word.

Maria She did.

Pete In seventeen years!

Maria *knees him in the balls. He recovers slowly.*

Maria Anything else?

Pete *sitting,* **Maria** *standing.*

Pete Yeah – least she exists.

Maria My mother lives in Canada.

Pete (*spits on the stove*) Fuckin' fairyland.

Maria Sent me a letter. You can tell where from, from the stamp. I looked it up – Canada. I memorised it – stamp, letter, his flob boilin' on the 'ot tile – like yours now.

Pete What d'you actually know about 'er?

Maria Nothin'. Not even a picture. 'Spect she didn't even speak English an' all the Italian I ever learn was filth an' lies. He told me she was dead, 'is young bride, the one 'e bought.

She takes a handful of money from the box and methodically begins to burn it in the flame of the stove. **Pete** *knocks it out of her hand and stamps on it.*

Pete No!

He examines it.

Look at it.

Beside himself with rage he smashes the carefully assembled shelter.

Maria You got a temper, in't ya?

Pete *stands in the ruins of his shelter.*

Pete Things ain't workin' out.

Maria No.

Pete Maybe you're right.

Maria (*looks over smashed camp*) 'Bout what?

Pete Leavin'.

Maria Oh!

Pete What d'you want, Maria? It ain't me, is it? It ain't ever been me. I'm going, I'm fuckin' goin'.

Maria *goes to* **Pete**.

Maria Where? (*Pause.*) You can't do nothing on your own. You got to be together.

Pete Like you and me?

Maria Remember my face? In the shop.

Pete (*pause*) He'd marked you.

Maria You walked in.

Pete Yeah.

Maria What a picture.

Pete He'd laid 'is 'ands on ya. Great blue mark.

Maria Yeah.

Pete *turns tentatively.*

Pete (*touching her face*) Looked so sore. And I could see you were tryin' not to cry. Your eyes were full with tears, and I could see you was bitin' your lip and fightin' to hold them back.

Maria Great welcome 'ome that was: Eileen for me mother and one in the mouth for losin' me virginity – 'e'd only just noticed – and then 'e made me stand there in the shop in me nylon pinny so's all the customers could see my shame. And then you walk in and start yellin' and screamin' and spittin'. I ain't never seen nothing like it. *Nobody* ever seen nothing like it.

Pete I was angry.

Maria You was. Made me think. But all them other people in the shop, they'll think about it too, and when they find out what 'appened to 'im, well . . . they'll think you 'ad something against 'im, something personal.

Pete Your face, it was what 'e done to your face. You know that –

Maria *I* know, but them others they don't, 'cause you was so angry you made no sense at all. Police'll look into it, they'll find out 'bout 'im and your mother and they'll say: that's why 'e done it.

Pete (*frightened*) Done what?

Maria Done 'im.

Pete No –

Maria When you left 'im –

Pete No –

Maria You notice if 'e was breathin'?

Pete 'Course 'e was –

Maria You sure?

Pete 'Course I'm –

Maria Looked? You looked? Made a point of it?

Pete No –

Maria There you are then. How d'you know if 'e was dead or alive?

Pete Dead? (*Pause.*) I stopped.

Maria Did ya? Second? Two seconds?

Pete 'E was breathin'.

Maria 'E was dyin'.

Pete *goes to cashbox and picks up money.*

Pete I just need . . . somethin' to tide me over.

Maria That's more than enough.

Pete 'Ere, take it. (*Holds out money.*)

Maria You ain't interested no more then?

Pete I don't want it. It's yours.

Maria You don't want to look after me no more then?

Pete All right?

Maria He's dead.

Pete (*moves downstage*) You weren't even there.

Maria (*behind* **Pete**) Telly in the corner, knocked over. Wound, here.

Pete (*turns to* **Maria**) I told ya that.

Maria *Exactly* here. (*Pause.*) I was in the garages across the street, watchin'.

Pete I didn't mean nuffin' like that to happen.

Maria Ah!

Pete It was –

Maria You . . . didn't lose hold of yourself or nothin'?

Pete You're lyin'.

Maria (*starts to move stage right*) If you like.

Pete You're *lyin'*.

Maria (*turns to* **Pete**) You got angry.

Pete This is nuffin' to do with me.

Maria 'Cause he laughed at you.

Pete I was frightened.

Maria And he laughed at you.

Pete What?

Maria Joke.

Pete 'E moved towards me.

Maria And you ran.

Pete I ran.

Maria Bringin' the box up into his face and he slid down.

Pete . . . like . . .

Maria . . . that cat does in them cartoons on the telly.

Pete Hung there, sort of . . .

Maria . . . slid down. Onto the floor.

Pete I had to leave! 'Fore 'e wakes up.

Maria Peter, people are fragile, they fall apart ever so easy.
Don't you know that? 'E was dyin' as you walked out the door.

Pete They'll go round and see me mother.

Maria Least of your worries now.

Pete Askin' things.

Maria Bound to.

Pete She 'ates that.

Maria *begins to move round the stage, thinking it out, talking.*

Maria Let's see. Sat'day night – Eileen? Got 'er own key. Mr

Pioli? (*Mimicked scream.*) Cars blockin' the street. Police crawlin' through the 'ouse puttin' things in plastic bags. (*Turns to* **Pete**.) Touch anything? No, you 'ad your rubber gloves on. Cameras flashin'. Chalk outline on the floor where 'e fell. The front page. *Murder!*

Pete I didn't –

Maria All them 'opes glowin' in 'is 'ead, then you come along. And they burn out. Oh, excellent! (**Pete** *drops money. Pause.*) *His* fuckin' 'opes. Night I come back, I 'ear 'em downstairs, 'im an' Eileen on the sofa – 'Oh, Mr Pioli. *Mr Pioli*'. Next morning it's side by side, ever so proper, and I can't believe what my ears is 'earin' cause 'e is goin' on about 'is 'appiness, 'is disappoint-ments. And then, right, and then 'e says 'Eileen . . . is gonna be your mother.' Eighteen years I been waitin' for my mother – 'er name, 'er face, 'er touch. Eighteen years I been askin', and what 'e finally comes up with is Eileen. (*To* **Pete**.) Murder. Well done.

Pete I could explain.

Maria *faces* **Pete**.

Maria 'Course: 'Sorry about that man I killed, officer'. 'Don't you worry, sir. He was only an Eyetie, after all.' Oh, Peter! When they get you in them cells, they're goin' to stick their truncheons right up your arse.

Silence. **Pete** *stumbles, stage right, and turns to* **Maria**.

Pete In the room . . . me hands . . . they wouldn't keep still.

Maria Nervous.

Pete Under the bed. Wasn't there.

Maria Must have moved it.

Pete You said! It's in the room under the bed. You fuckin' said.

Maria Should have been.

Pete I stripped it off – everything.

Maria The curtains was open.

Pete Nothin' there.

Maria Should have closed the curtains like I told ya.

Pete I was terrified. Out of my fuckin' brain.

Maria He come back for somethin', didn't he? Forgot somethin'. Bad memory.

Pete Then the wardrobe. Pulled it out, all of it.

Maria Fuck your memory.

Pete Chest of drawers.

Maria Fuck you, Giovanni.

Pete One after the other.

Maria *gets down from the ledge, wide sweep stage left.*

Maria Lookin' through his pockets for the house key. Never remembers which pocket, but it's always there somewhere. Yeah, it's always there. (*To* **Pete**.) Opens the door . . . and hears ya.

Pete I know. Oh fucking no! I was . . .

Maria Leaves the door wide open and goes through.

Pete I was out. I just . . .

Maria Into the living room.

Pete Down the stairs.

Maria Out of sight.

Pete And *go*.

Silence.

(*Quiet.*) I . . . must have hit him. Little drop of blood makin' its way out of his nose and down the side of his mouth . . . and a thin red path where it's been. (*Pause.* **Pete** *turns to* **Maria**.) What happened?

Maria The front door was wide open. I had to go over. And I just had to go inside, couldn't resist it. There he was. All the swagger knocked out of him. All the Neapolitan bollocks. Looked relaxed. (**Maria** *drops down to* **Giovanni**.) Almost friendly. (*She kneels.*) His hand was soft. I never remembered his hands soft . . . white. Papa? (*Pause.*) And he opens his eyes.

Pete (*relief*) He was breathing.

Maria 'Maria'. There I am swimming in the mist. 'Maria?' Where is she, Papa? Me mother. Where is she? 'Nowhere, she's nowhere.' I have to know where she is, Papa, it's time for me to know, I come back for it, I need it. You see, this life, this what you give me is no good. It's too thin. It's too cold.

Pete Oh Gawd.

Maria There's nothing to feed my mind.

Pete She's off her 'ead. She's off her fucking 'ead.

Maria I told him. What I'd never told him before. All the things I done – I don't know: run off, fucked about, everything – but I never told him how I felt, and I felt it *years*. I'm not real. I'm not a person. I'm cunt. That's all. This little cunt who works in the winders. Winder dressing. (*Pause.*) And then one day *she's* there in me mind. I can feel her fear. And suddenly I'm seeing everything through her eyes: grease on the shop winder, paper peelin' off the wall, damp yeller formica. England. She don't speak a word of it. England, where he brought her. And him. I can see Giovanni too, through her eyes: that straight, cock-backed stand on him, them skin-purse pig's eyes, and there, even there at the very beginning she hates him. But there's never been any choice for it. No, nothing but him night after night – his breath, his hands, his weight, his pig's weight forcing its way inside. (*Pause.*) Suddenly she's there in me mind. 'Course, that's the end of me student. And the flat, and all that. I get a bit . . . unreliable.

She stares into space.

Pete Maria?

Maria I explained it to him. Papa, I said, I told 'im – I 'ad a sort of vision. Somebody wanked all down the winder and I saw everythin'.

Pete What did 'e say?

Maria After that, I had to come back then, didn't I? I mean, once I believed in her. I had to come back and make him tell me where she was. So I asked 'im.

Pete Yeah?

Maria Where she was.

Pete Well?

Maria (*pause*) And you got to have money to go to Canada. That's why I wanted it. Besides, I thought: the box, there may be something there, a photo maybe. An address.

She looks at the marriage certificate.

Francesca Madrianni.

Pete He wouldn't say nothing? He was . . . (*Slumps.*) What are we going to do?

Maria I thought you was going?

Pete Nowhere to go, is there? Not on me own. (*Pause.*) And you don't want nothing more to do with me, do ya? (*Pause.*) Do ya? (*Pause.*) Why d'you pick on me?

Maria 'Cause your eyes shine when you look at me, like they're doing now, and I knew I could make you do anything I wanted.

Pete Didn't you –

Maria What else did you have to do? And I liked it, you being angry for me. Made me feel like I was there. You didn't just look through me. Canada.

Pete 'E tell you where in Canada?

Maria No. (*Drops the imaginary hand.*) Goodbye, Papa. The key was in his pocket.

She gets to her feet and starts to pack.

Pete He didn't say nothing, then? (*Pause.*) What you doing?

Maria Told ya. I ain't staying here freeze to death.

Pete It's thousands of miles away.

Maria So? Look, Peter, look at where we are. What's this like, eh? This ain't like you remembered Peter; ain't the place of your dreams is it? It's cold, it's empty and there has to be something better. (*Picks up 'Teach Yourself Italian'.*) And I got some learning to do.

Pete They don't speak Italian there.

Maria My mother speaks Italian everywhere.

Pete If she's still alive.

Maria I know she is, I know, I can tell. I'll tell you how. (**Pete** *holds up his hands to stop her.*) When I was a little girl, go to church every Sunday and look at this picture – lady with black hair and a white dress. Stare at it for a long, long time, and this voice says: 'An angel in Heaven. Just like your mother'. But even as my father says the words the sunlight bursts in the winder. Strong and warm and just a little bit certain. (*She is ready to go.*) Well?

Pete Sleeping bag – what about the next time?

Maria (*moves towards* **Pete** *a little*) We'll go down the coast and sneak aboard a ship, hide in a lifeboat and slowly fuck our way across the Atlantic. How about that? (*Pause.*) Tell you a story.

Pete (*takes a little step forward*) Piss off. No more stories. If you're gonna go, just . . . go.

Maria When me student got bored with me an' kicked me out and I 'ad to come back 'ome, walking up the steps at Catford Bridge Station, what's the first thing I see when I come out into the light? Saturday afternoon, broad daylight? You, leaning over the bridge, watchin' the trains, and crying. Great tears like pearls rolling down your cheeks. All these people walking past and there you was crying your 'eart out on the trains. Didn't understand it then, but that didn't matter. I thought: yes, there's

somebody else, there's somebody else. (*Pause.*) Suit yourself.
Arrivederci.

*She goes. He is turned away from her. Finally he turns to look after her.
He can't see her.*

Pete Maria?

Blackout.

Methuen New Theatrescripts series offers frontline intelligence of the most original and exciting work from the fringe:

authors in the same series

Karim Alrawi
Iraj Jannatie Ataie
Harwant S Bains
Aphra Behn
Edward Bond
Howard Brenton
Mikhail Bulgakov
Bob Carlton
Jim Cartwright
Caryl Churchill
Tony Craze, Ron Hart,
Johnnie Quarrell
Sarah Daniels
Nick Darke
Nick Dear
David Edgar
Harvey Fierstein
Peter Flannery
Peter Gibbs
Andre Gregory
Robert Holman
Kevin Hood
Debbie Horsfield
Dusty Hughes
Ron Hutchison
Tunde Ikoli
Terry Johnson
Charlotte Keatley
Manfred Karge
Barrie Keeffe
Paul Kember
Thomas Kilroy
David Lan

Deborah Levy
Kate Lock
Stephen Lowe
Doug Lucie
David Mamet
Tony Marchant
Philip Massinger
Mustapha Matura
Marlane Meyer
Michael Meyer
Anthony Minghella
Adrian Mitchell
Gregory Motton
Tom Murphy
G F Newman
Louise Page
Stephen Poliakoff
Christina Reid
Rob Ritchie
David Rudkin
William Saroyan
Ntozake Shange
Wallace Shawn
Jack Shepherd
David Spencer
C P Taylor
Sue Townsend
Michelene Wandor &
Mike Alfreds
Timberlake Wertenbaker
Peter Whelan
Michael Wilcox
Nicholas Wright

The Astronomer's Garden
and
Beached

The Astronomer's Garden 'While its base is the vicious rivalry between Astronomer Royal Flamsteed and Halley calculating longitude, its true subjects are sex, class and the real world they cannot catalogue. Hood paints the two, irresistibly, as bombastic old sticks, but the play's real strength is its exploration of relationships, showing how Flamsteed's wife and maid navigate male ego-infested waters.'

Sarah Hemming, *Independent*

'In **Beached** a couple of young runaways, cast up on the beach of a bird sanctuary, cling to the wreckage of their lives and try to construct some kind of future from the fragments of their emotionally and physically brutalised pasts. Harsh, tender and moving.'

Helen Rose, *Time Out*

Kevin Hood's plays include **Beached** (Croydon Warehouse, 1987), **The Astronomer's Garden** (Croydon Warehouse, 1988) and **Sugar Hill Blues** (Croydon Warehouse, 1990).